Hot Air Balloon Coloring Book For Grown Ups

This Air Balloon Coloring book belongs to:

____

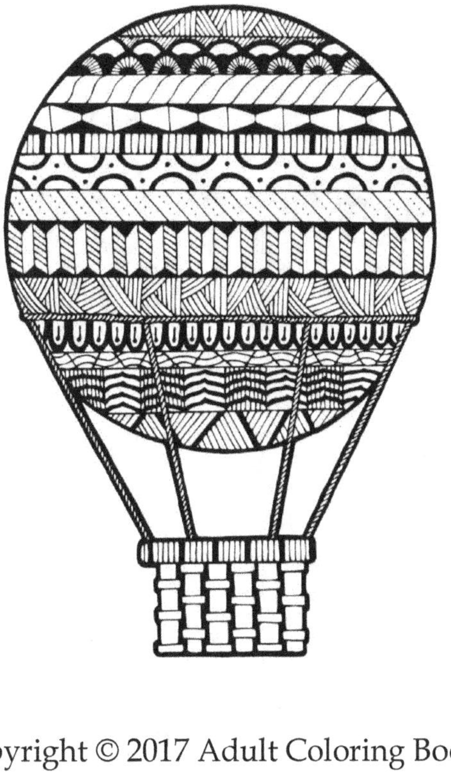

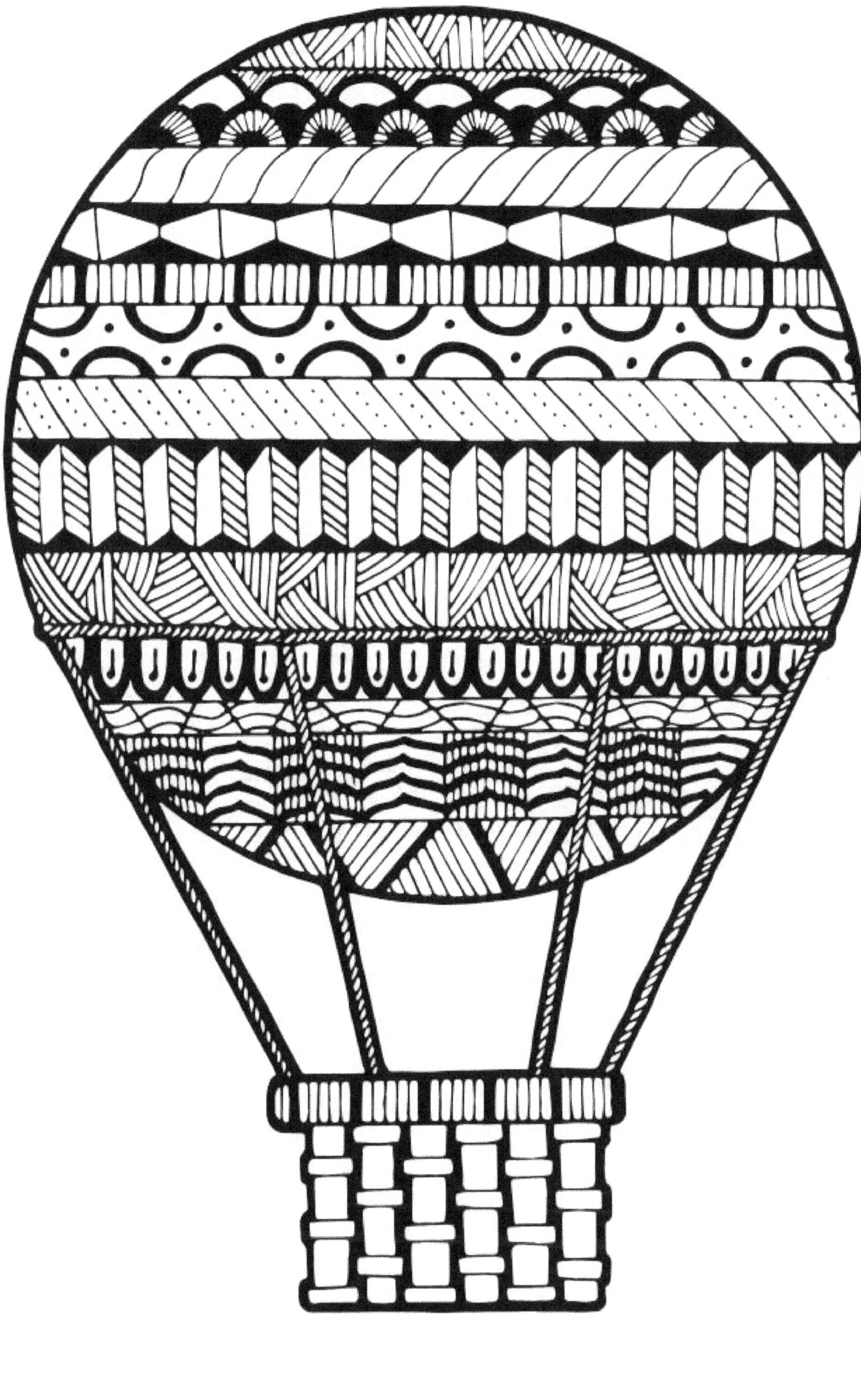

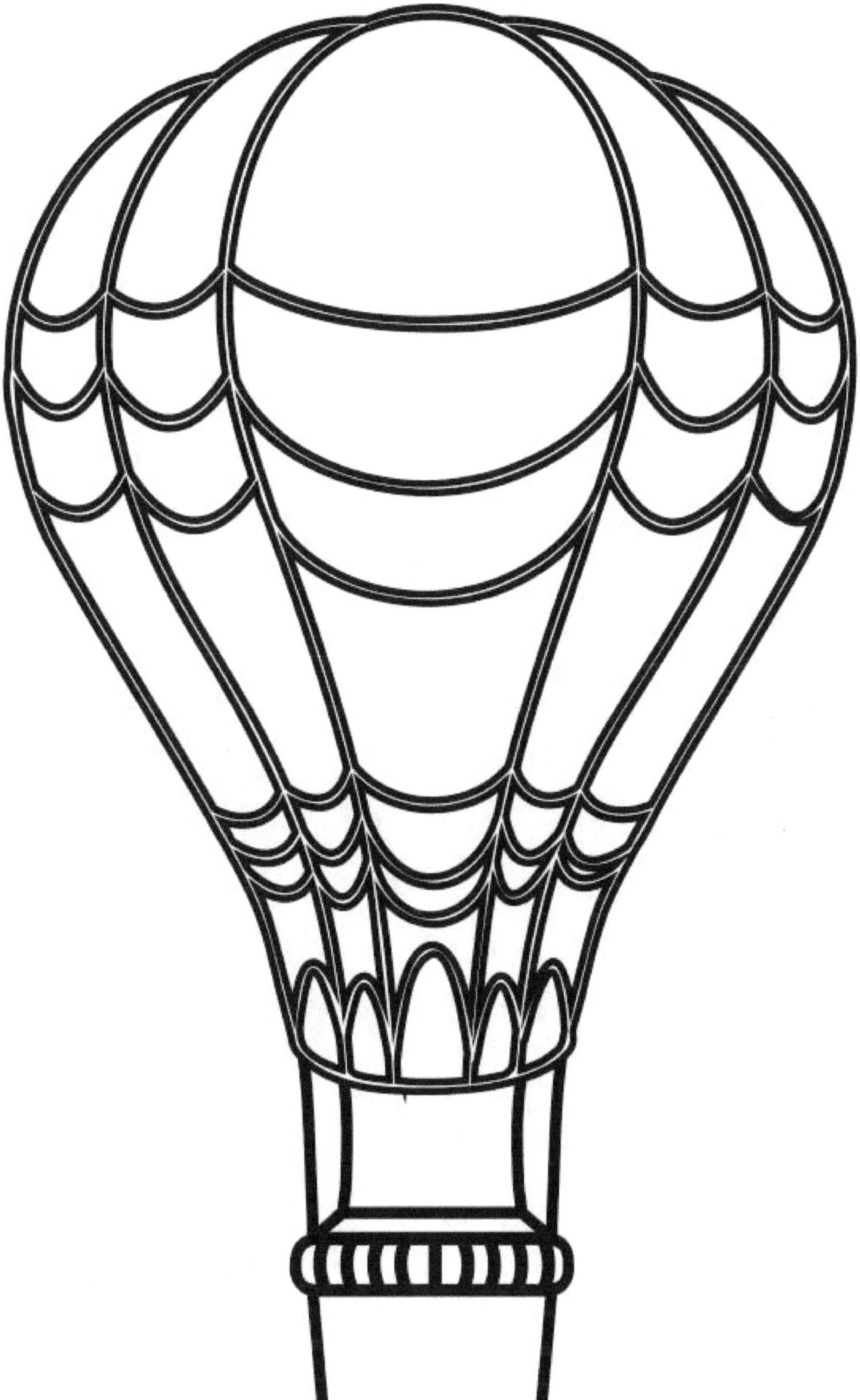

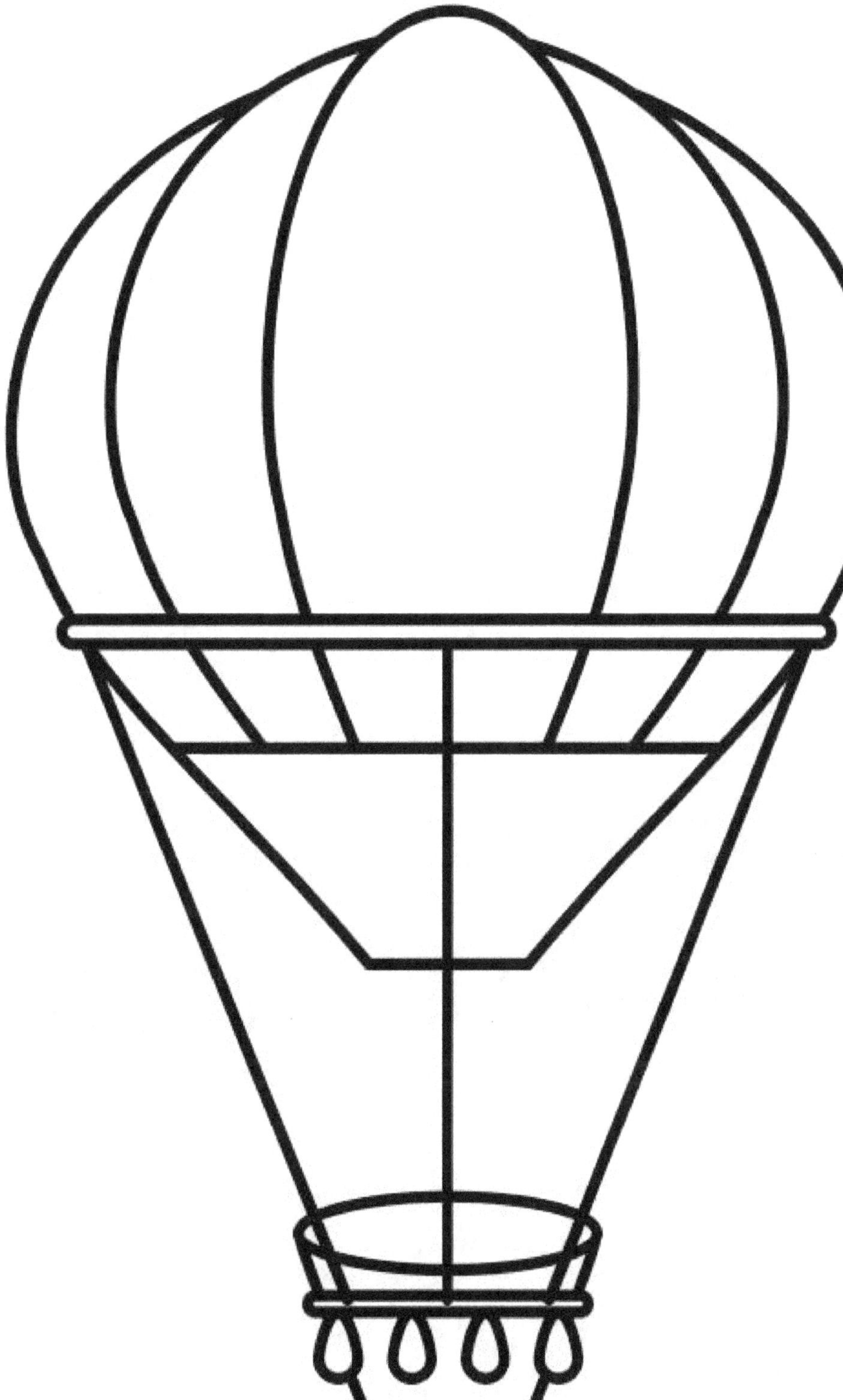

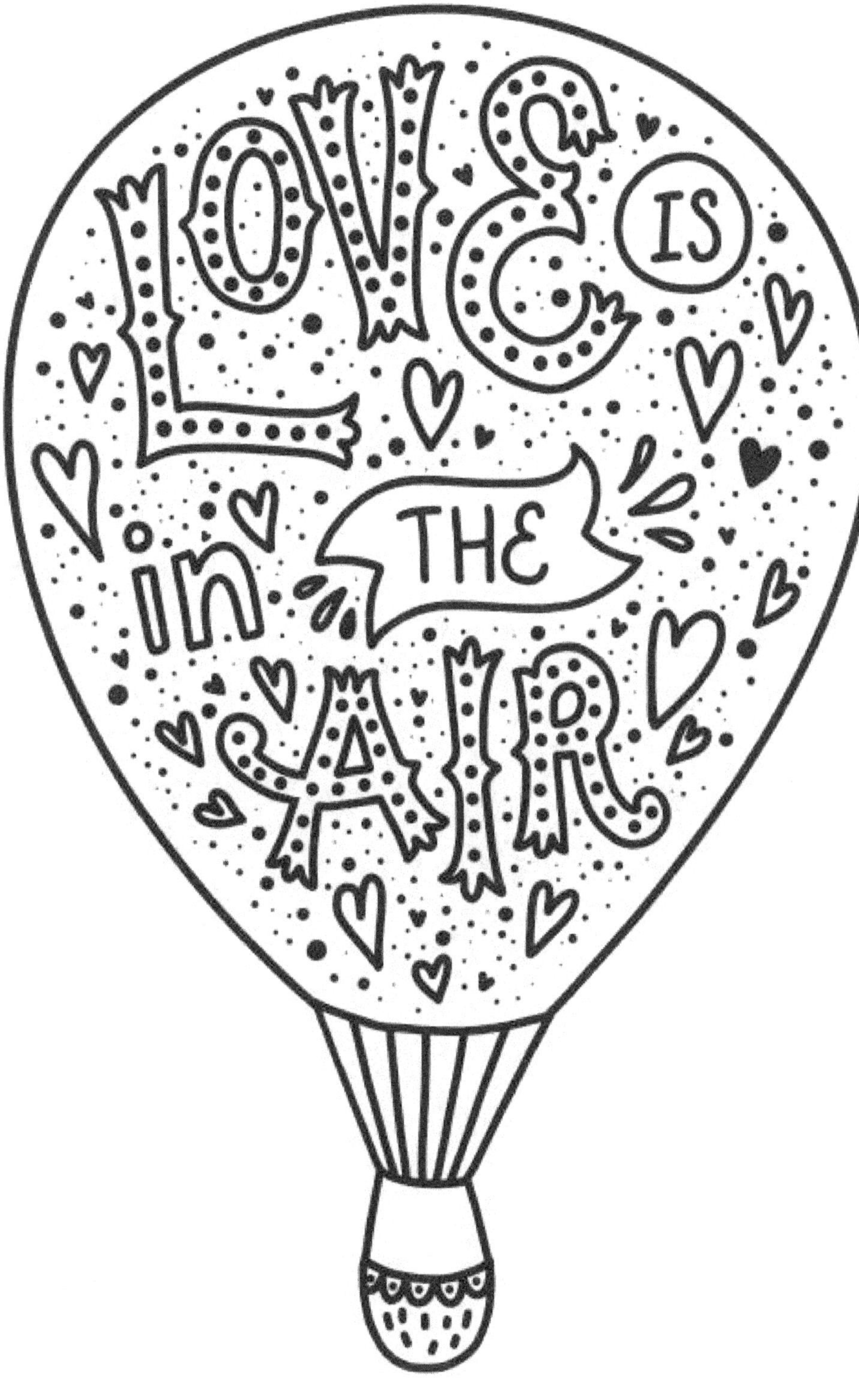
LOVE IS
in THE
AIR

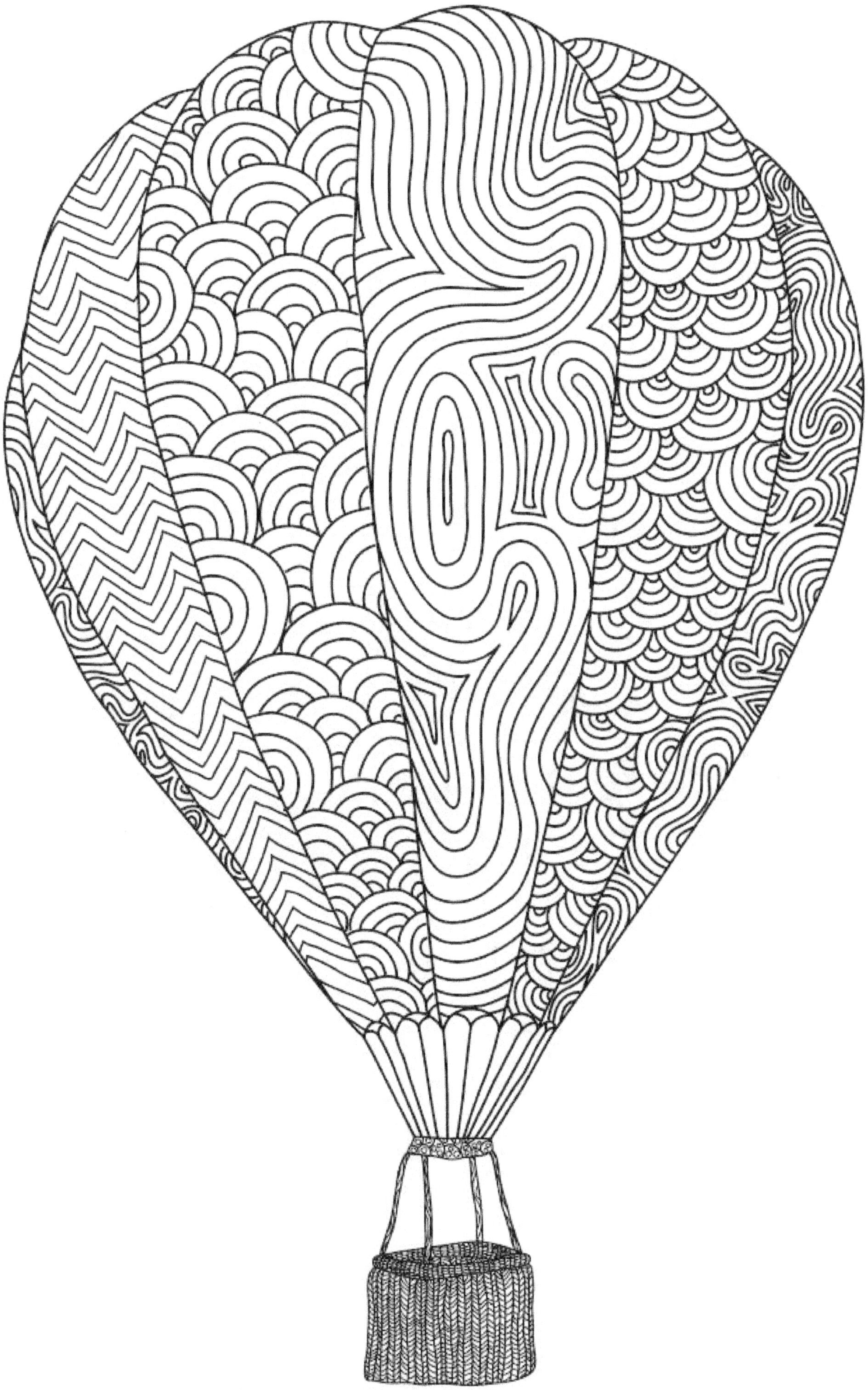

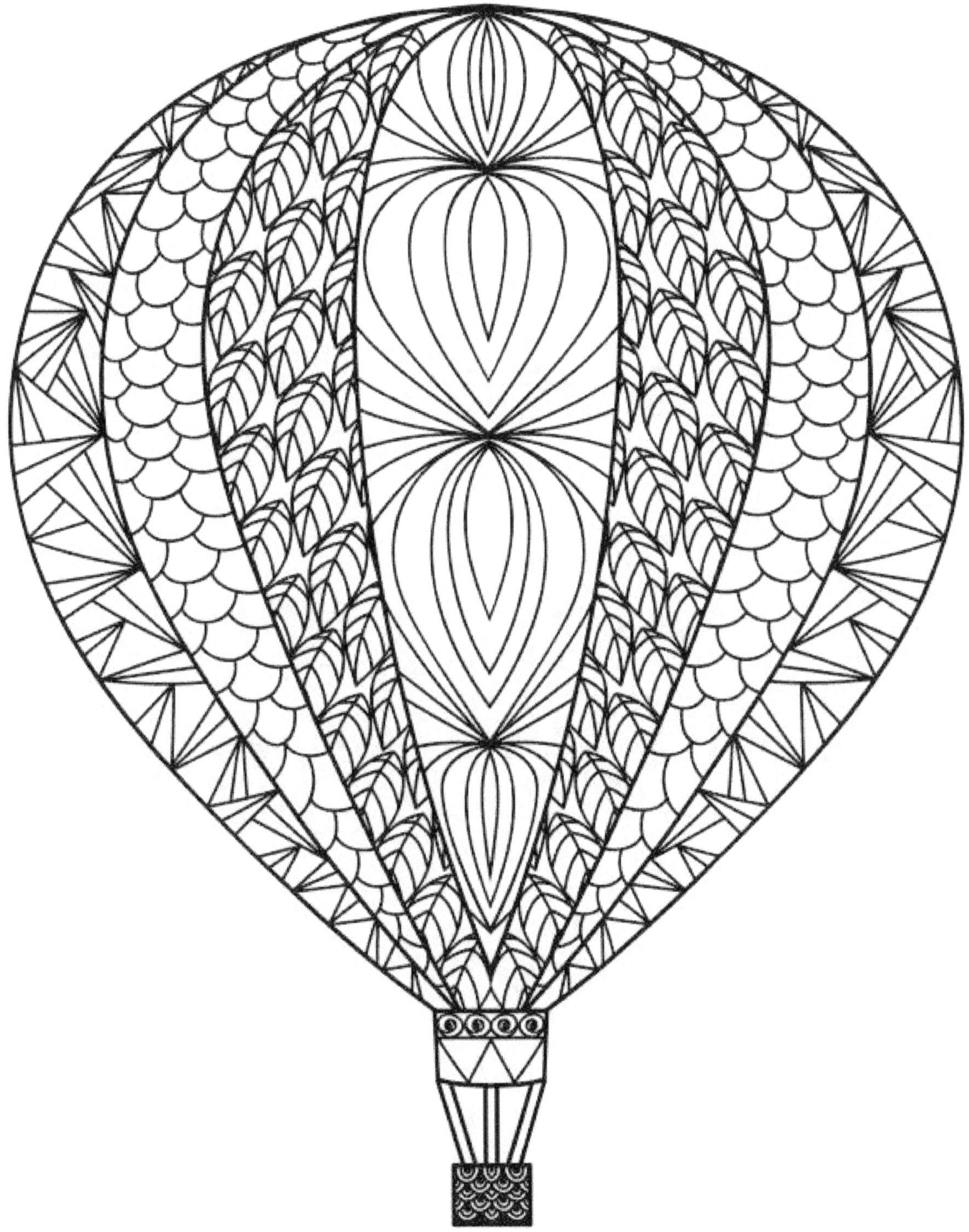

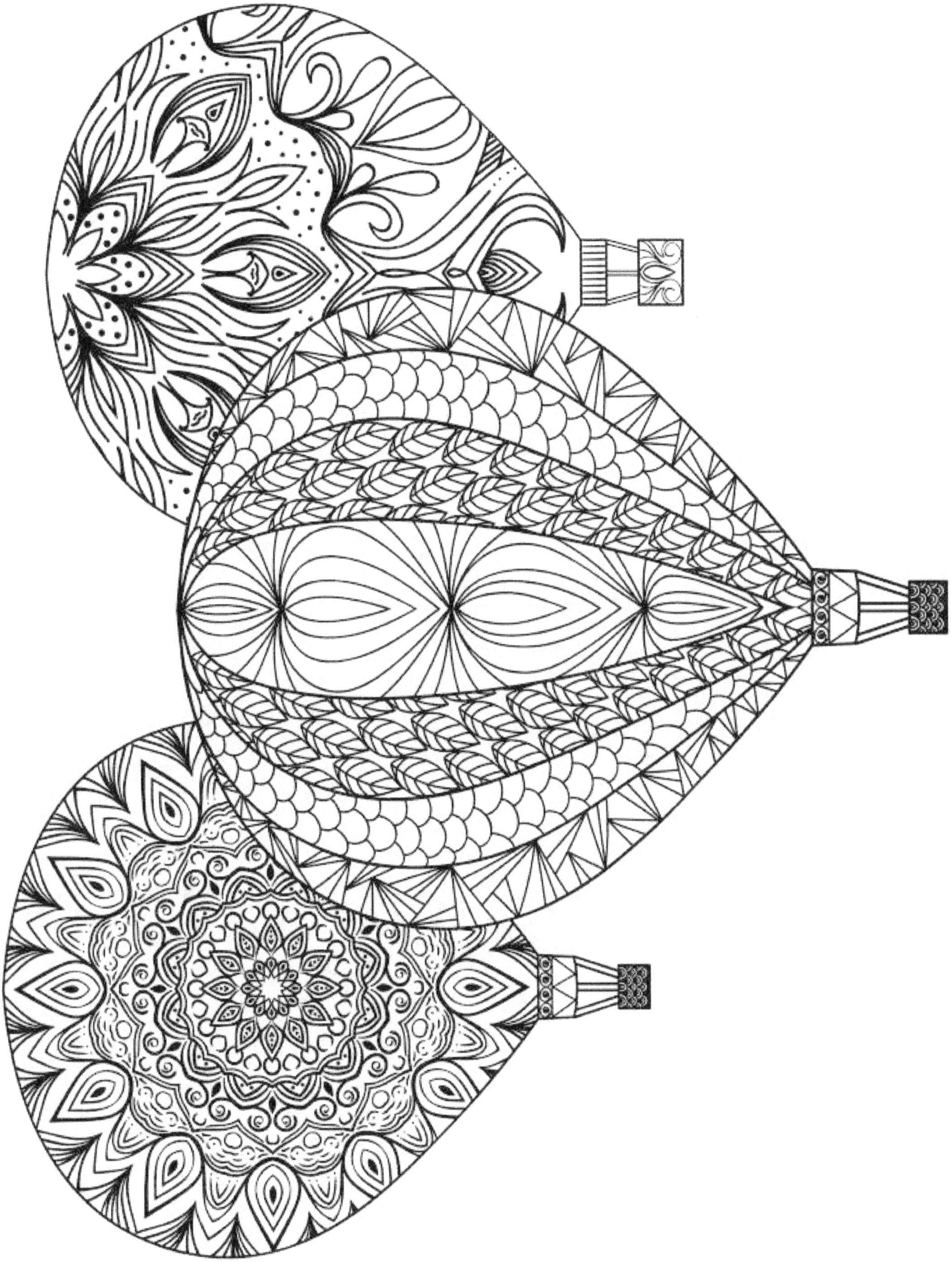

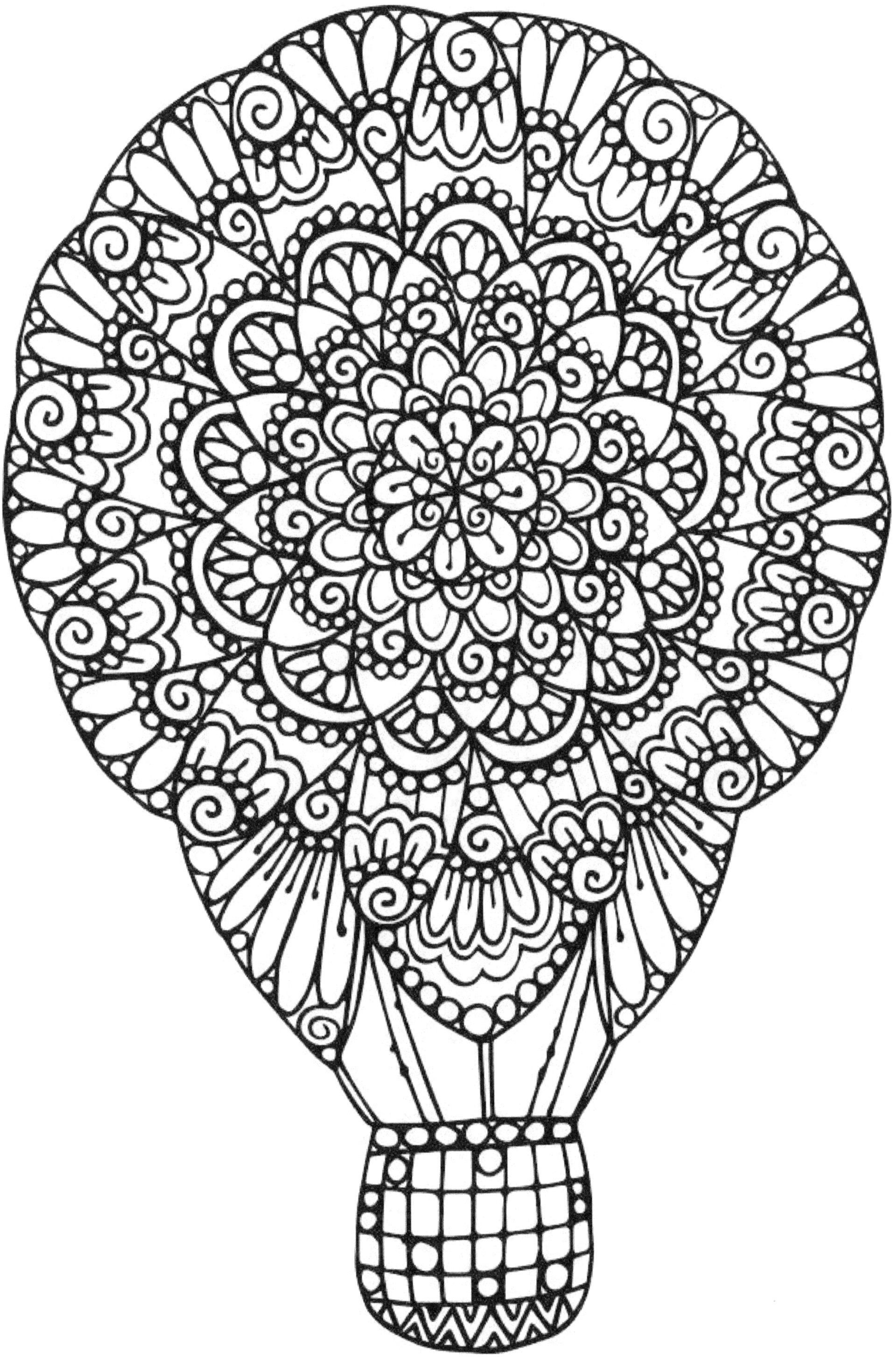

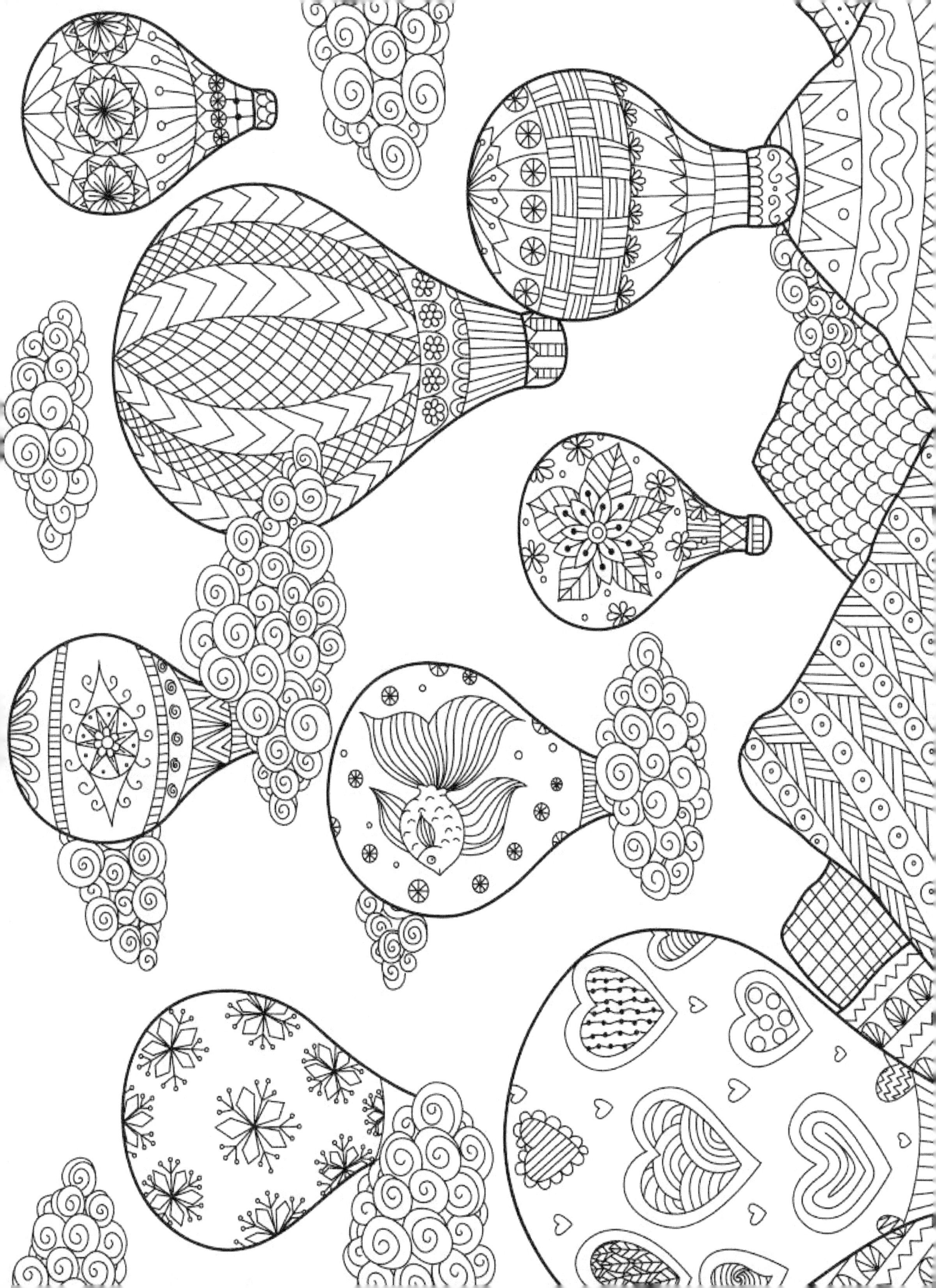

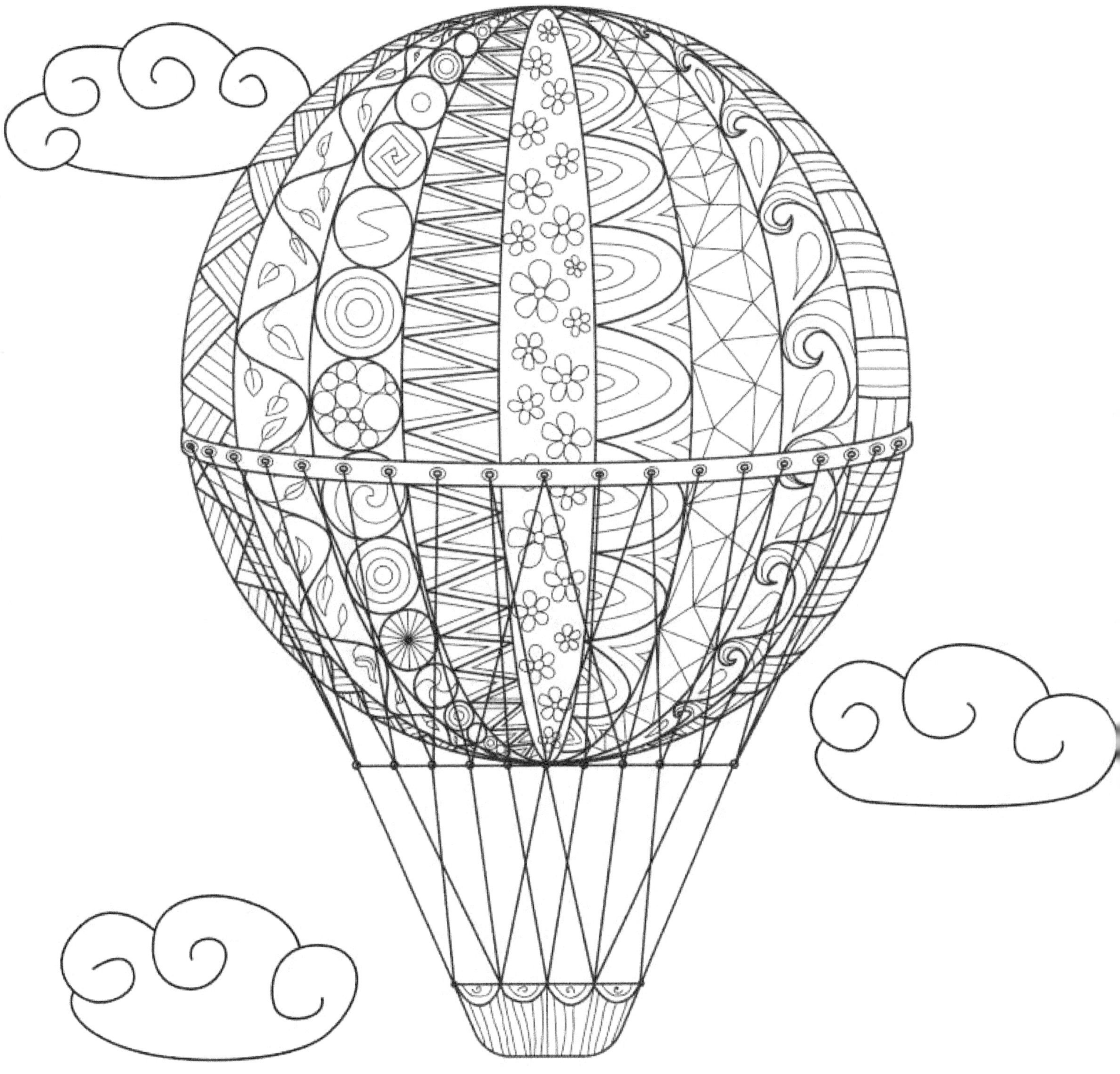

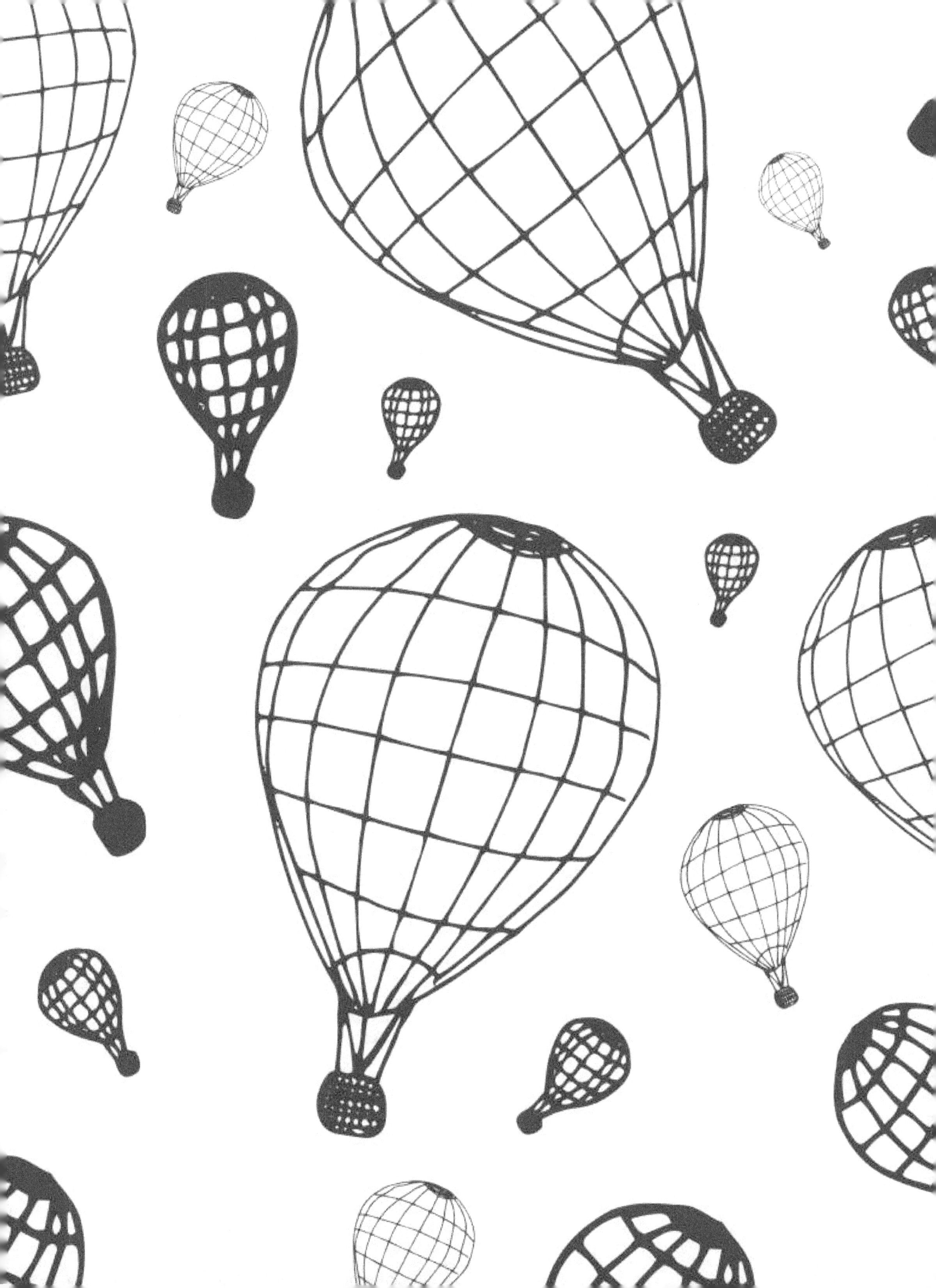

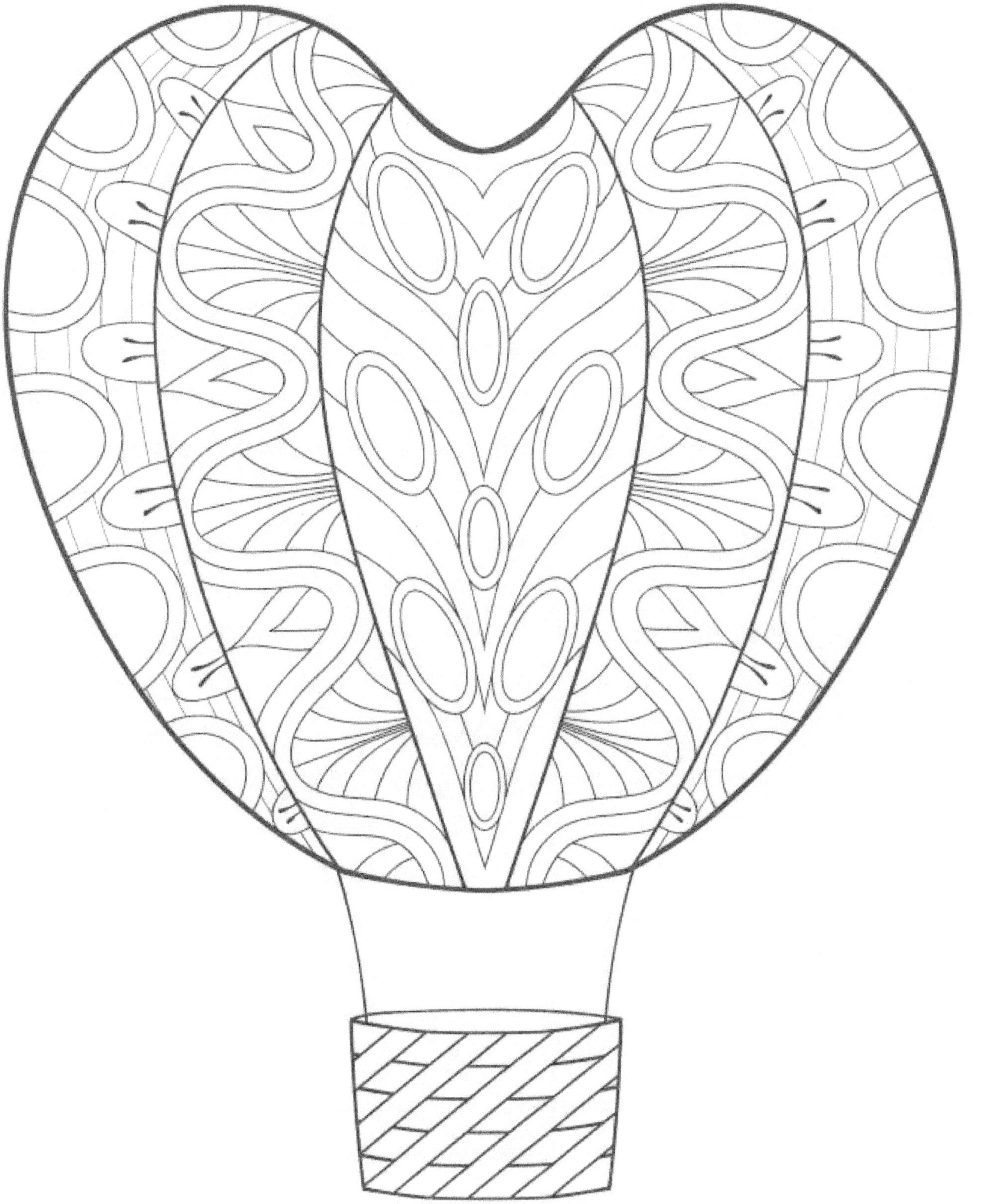

Bonus Frogs and Sea Turtles Coloring Pages.

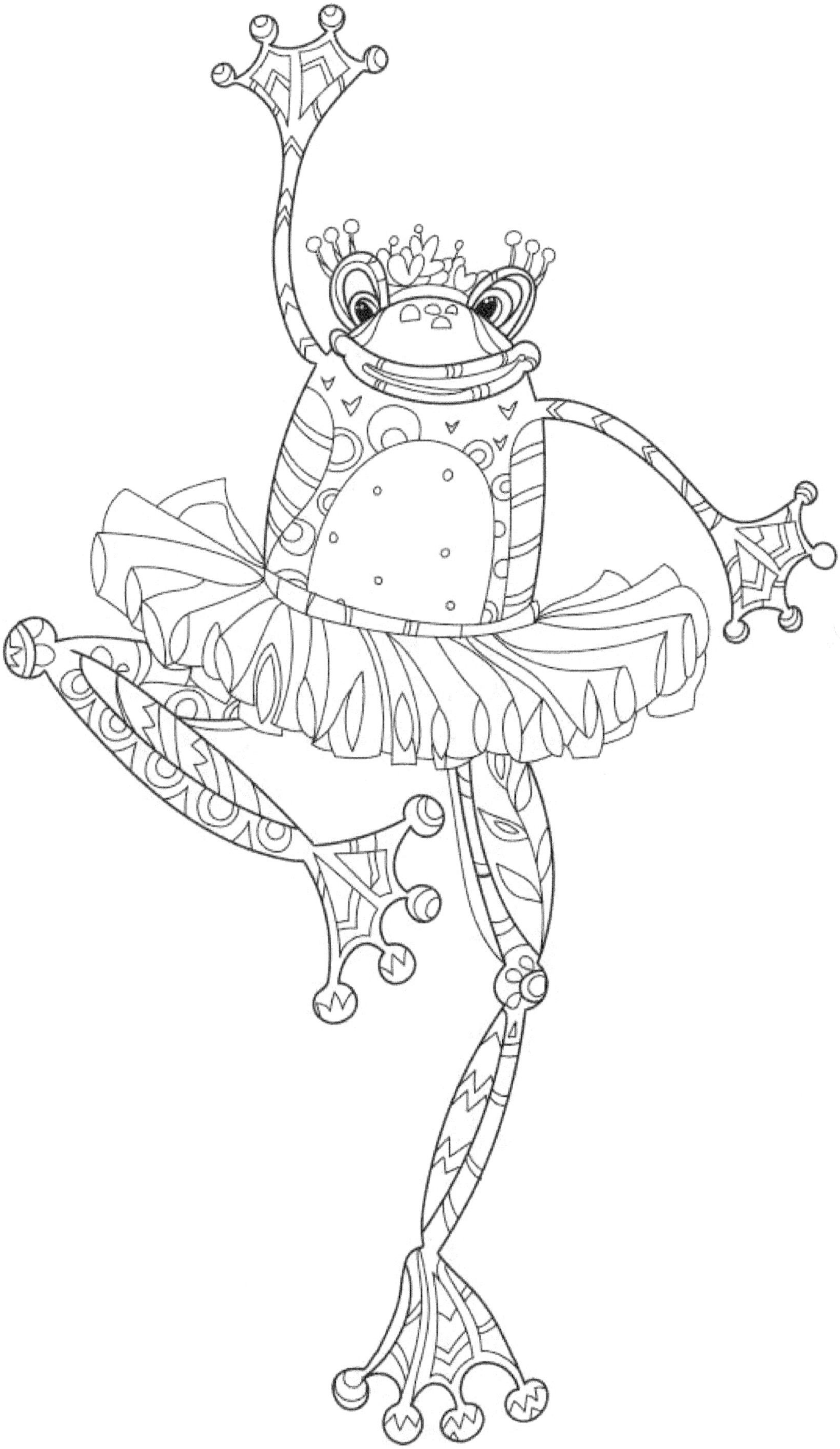

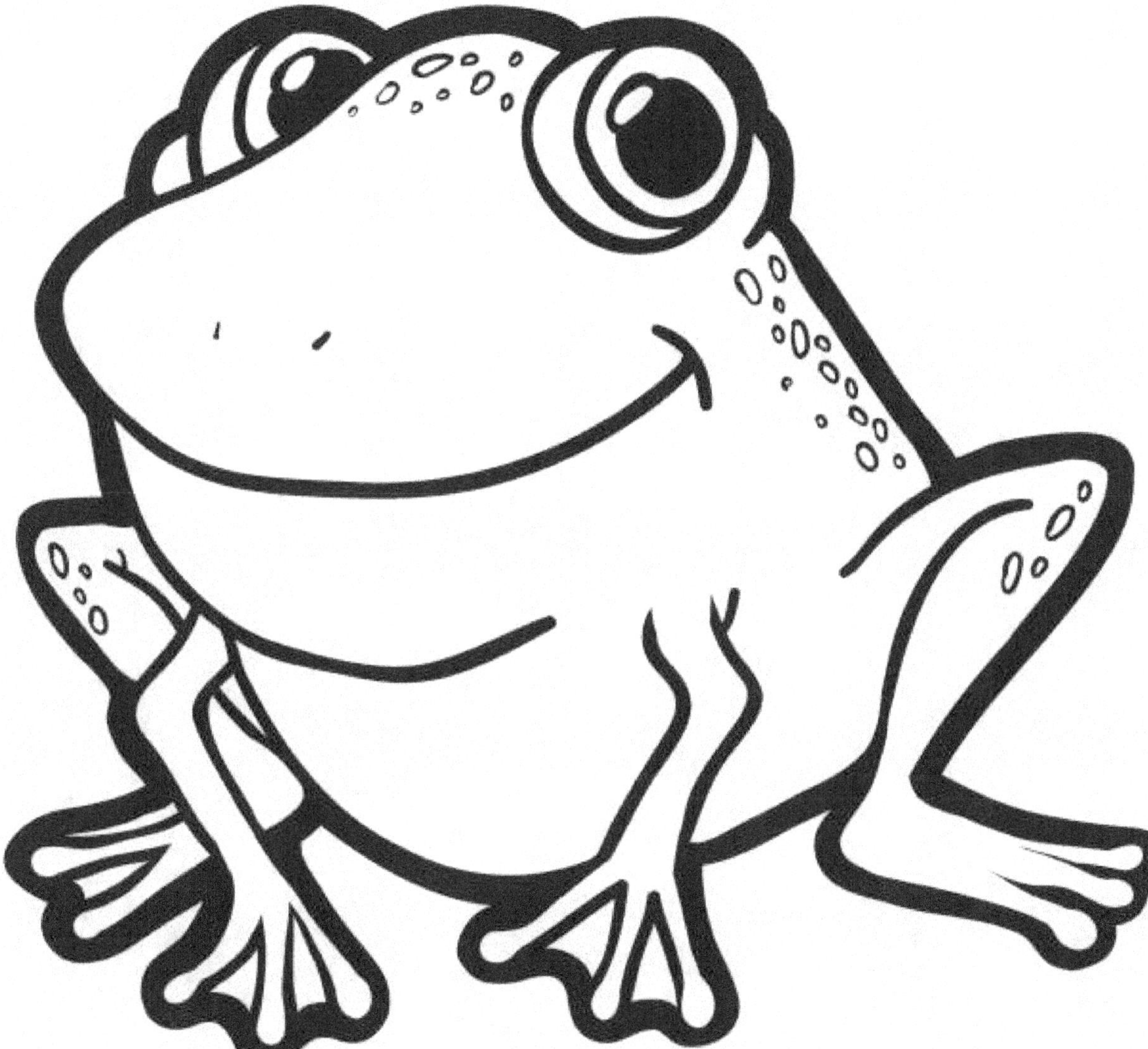

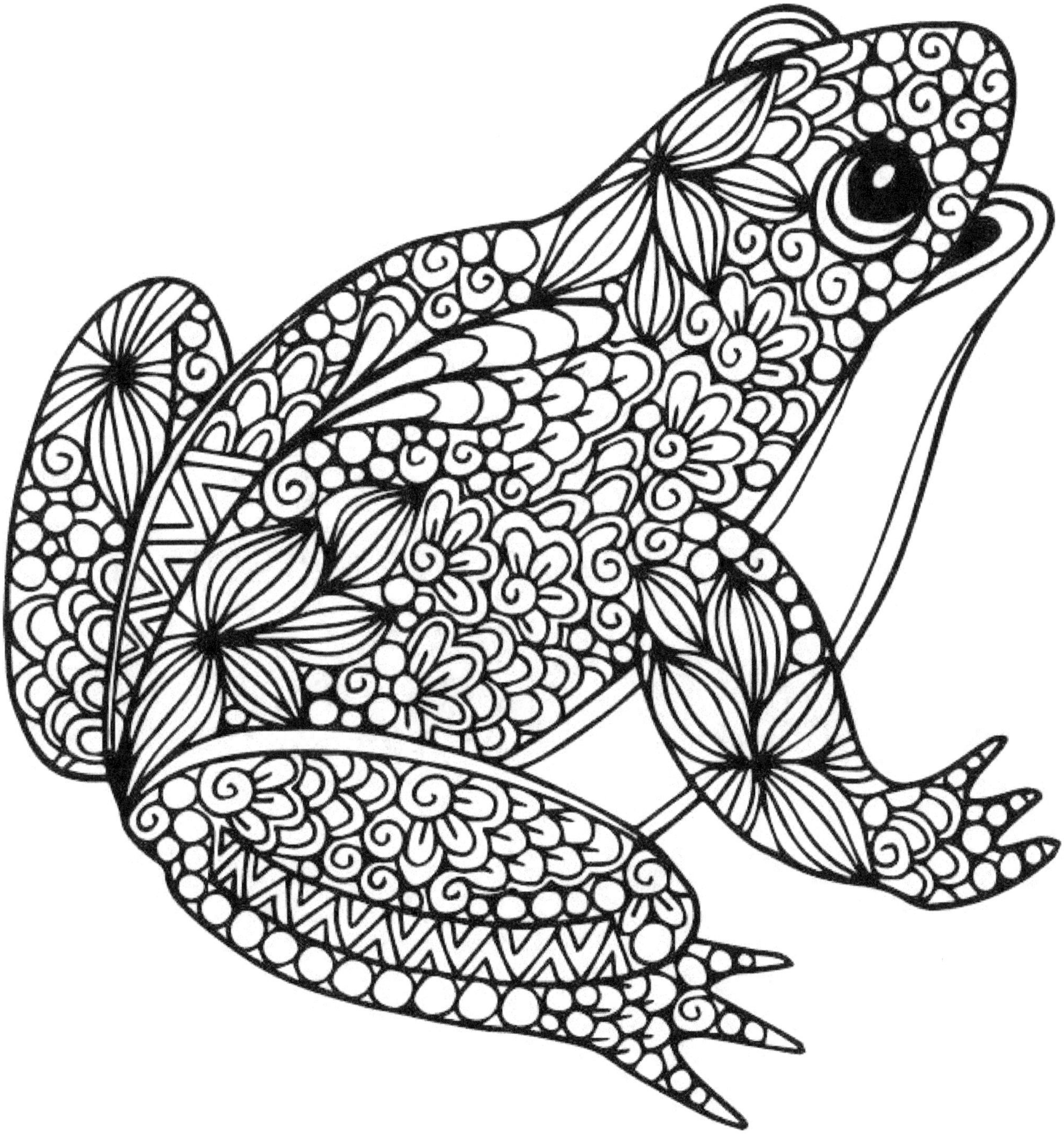

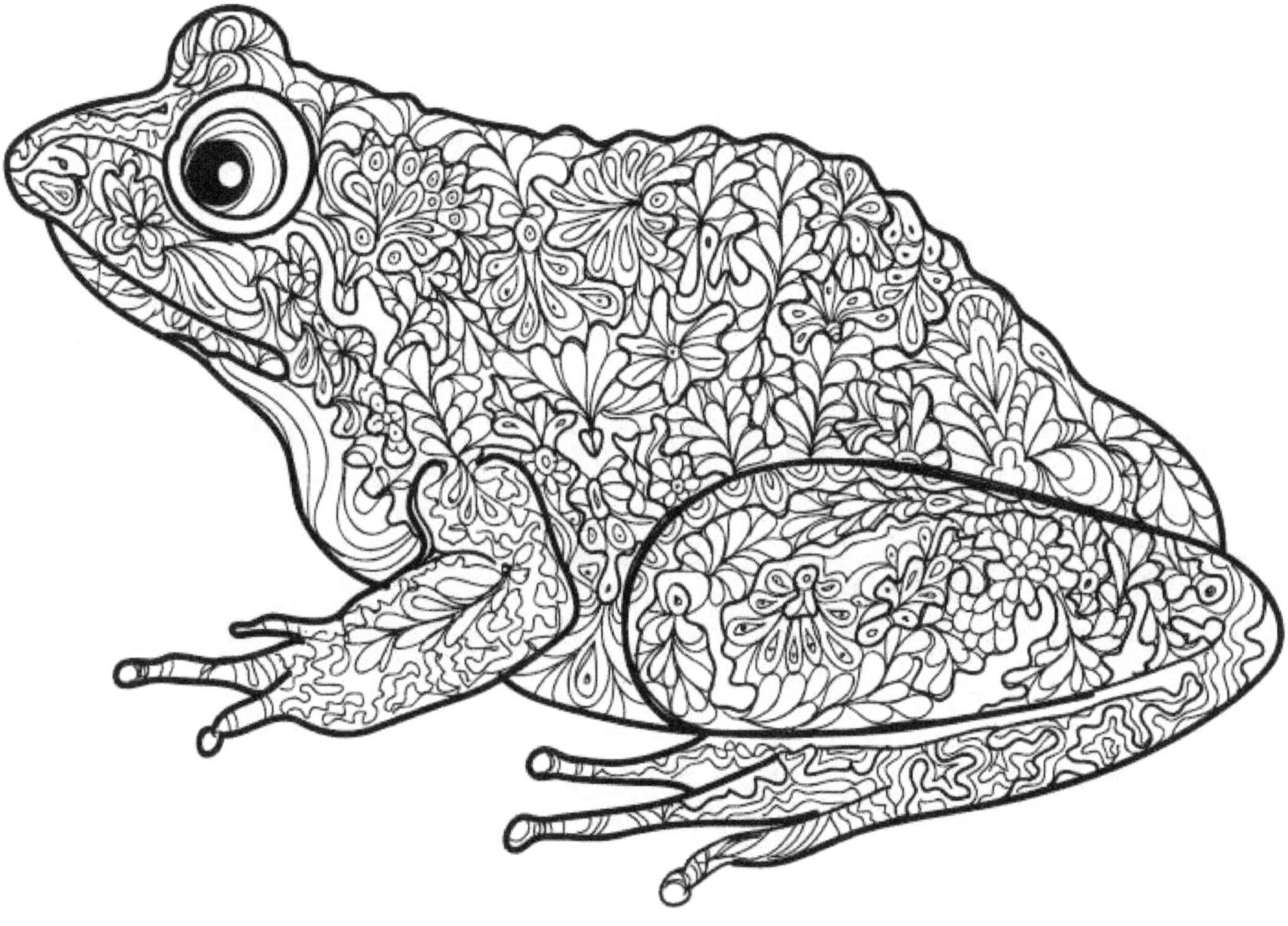

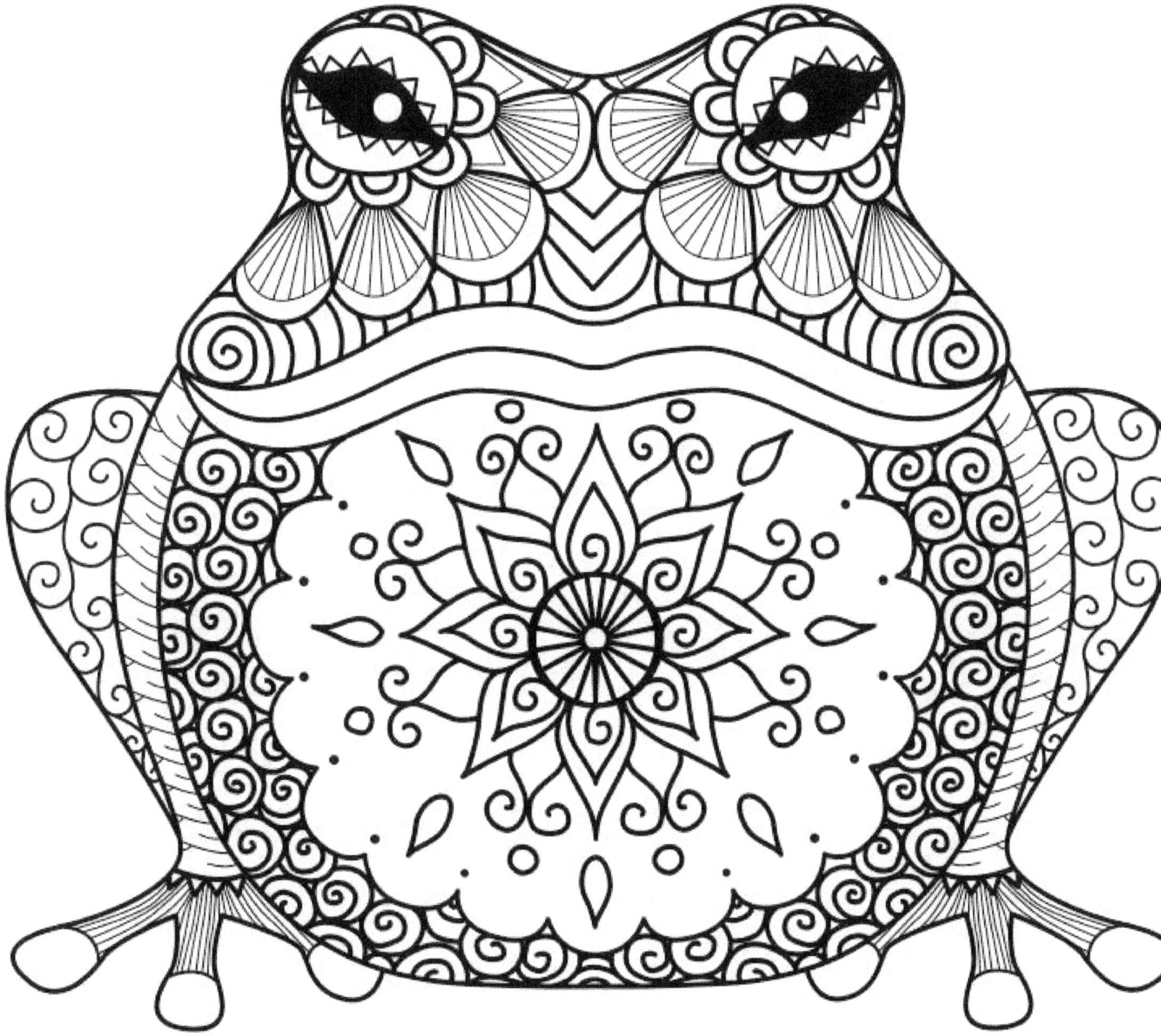

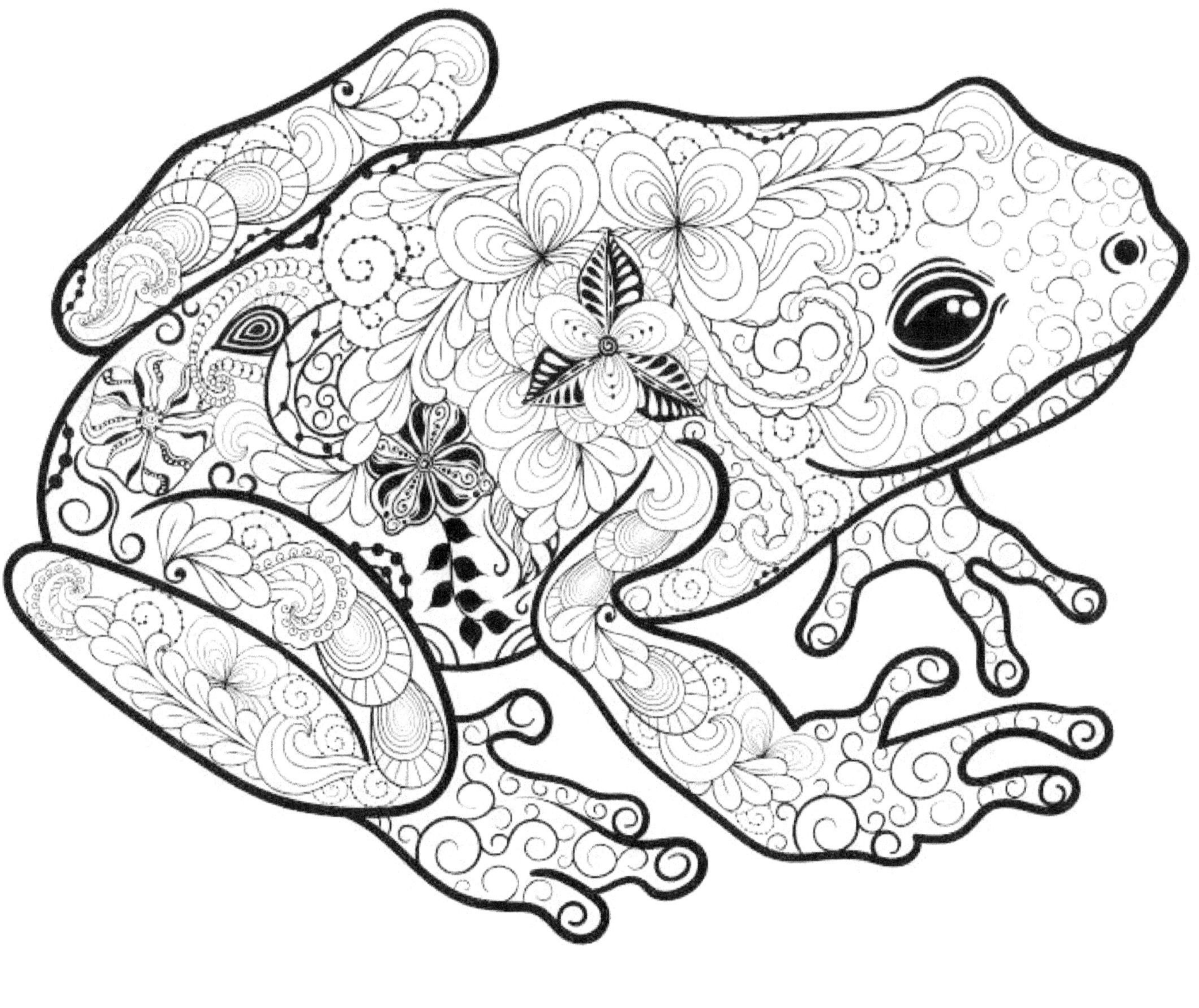

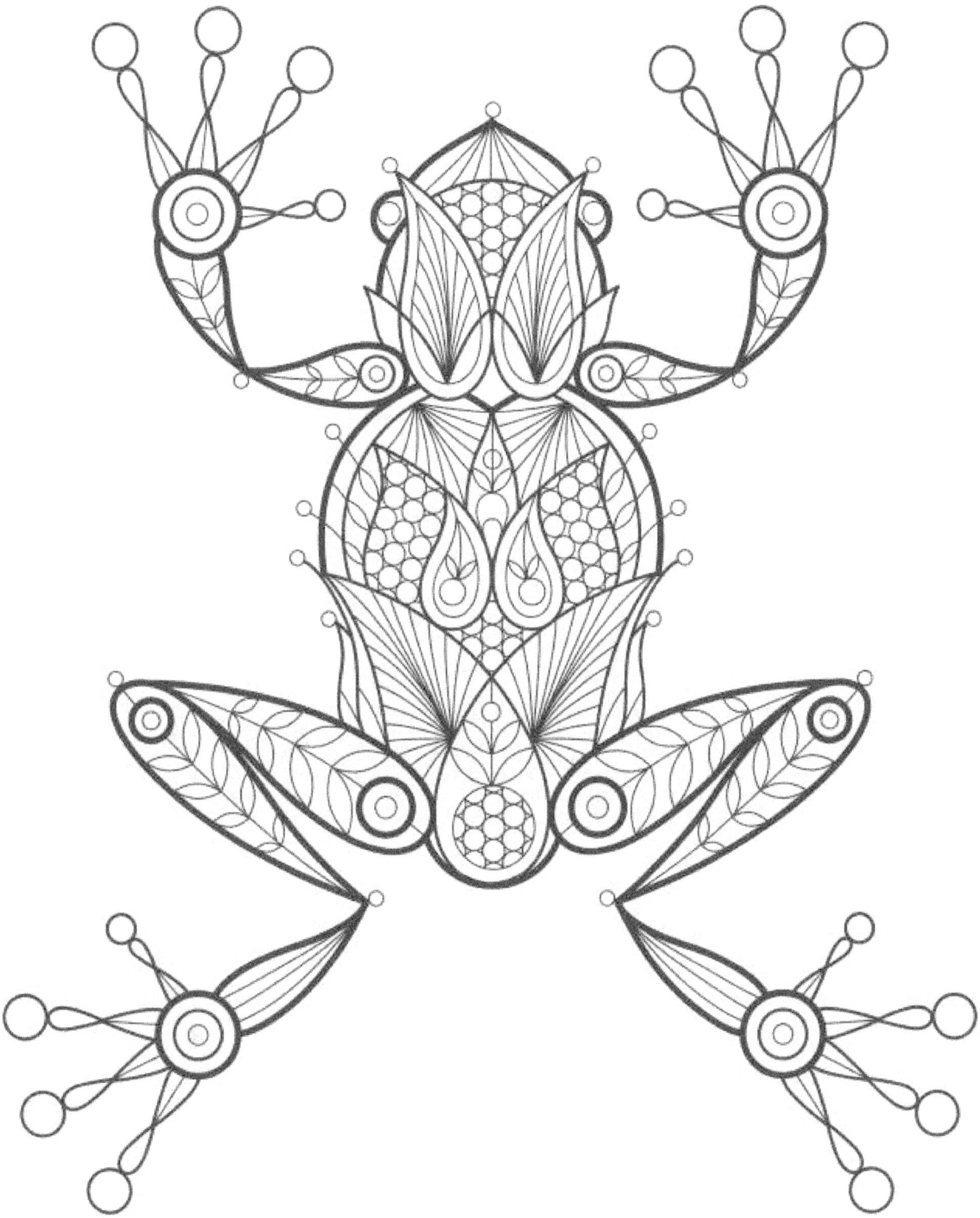

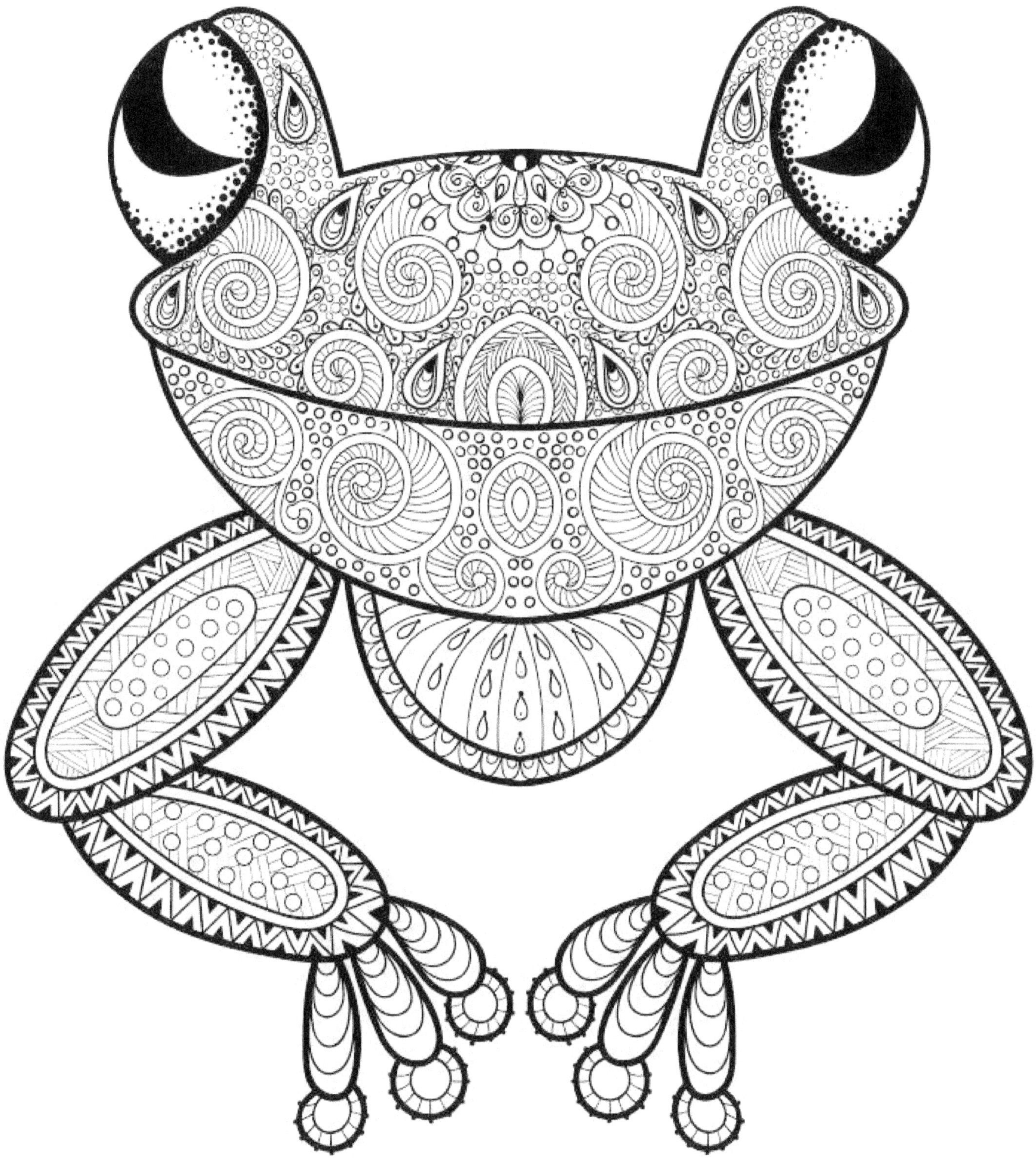

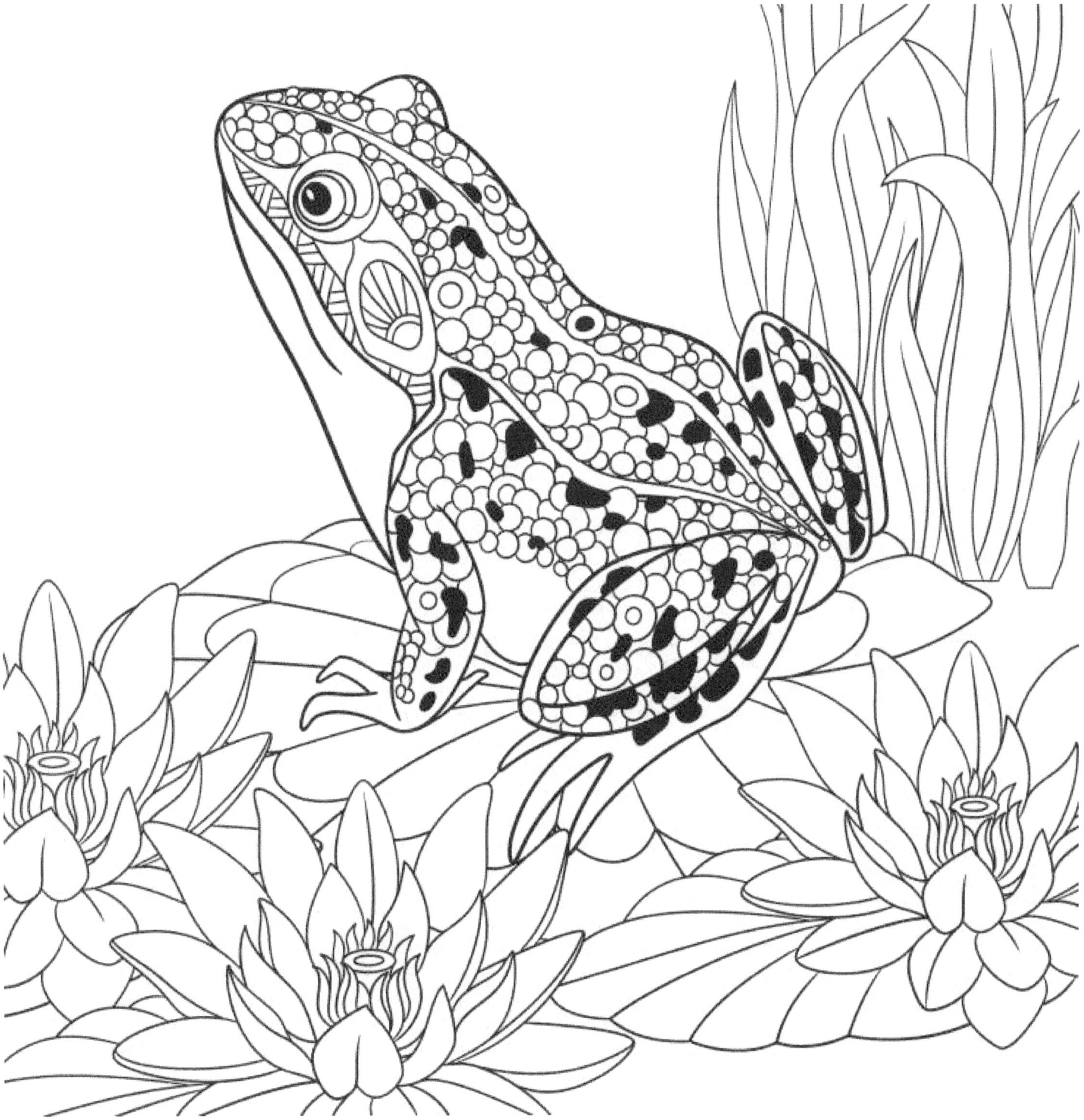

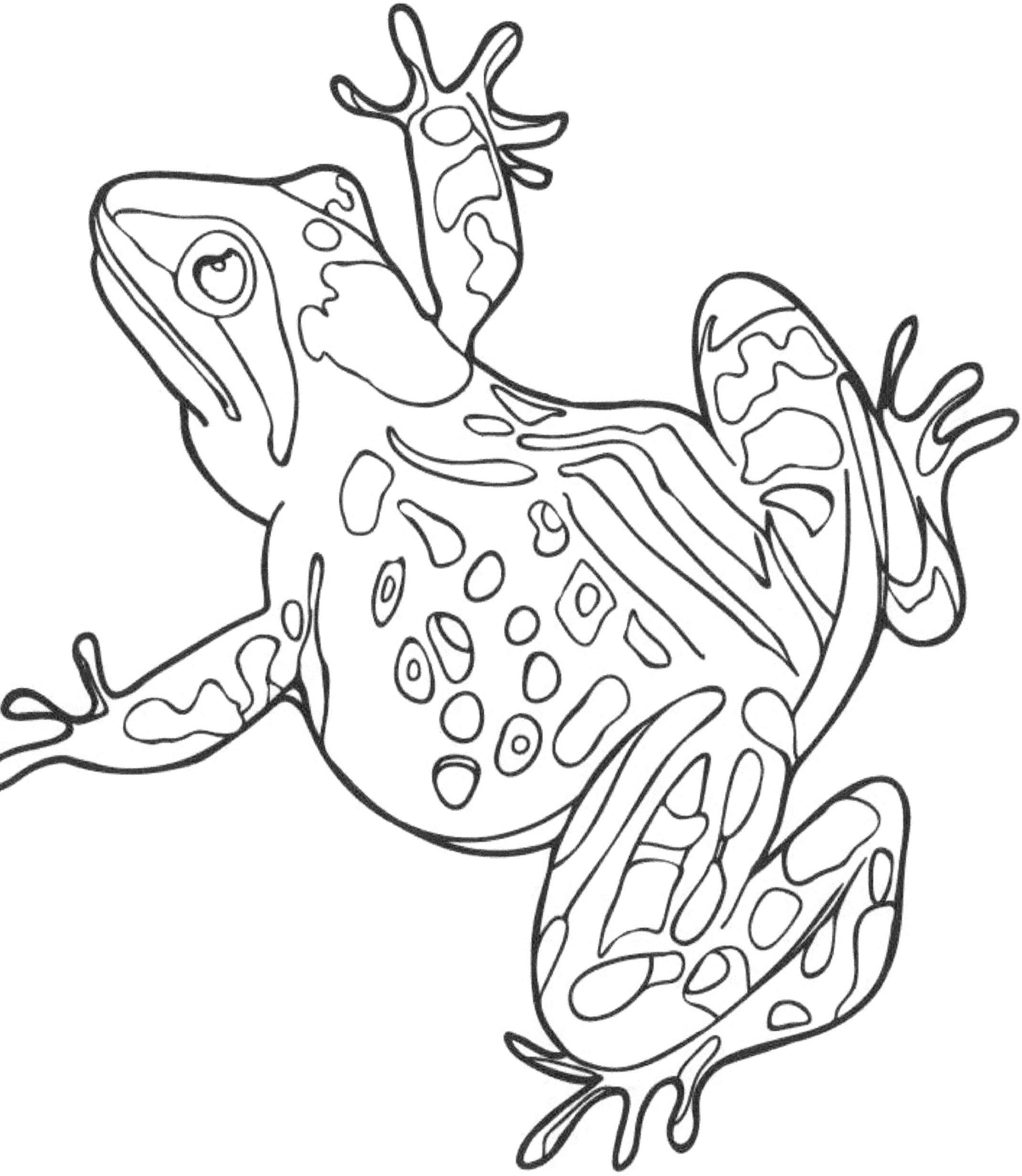

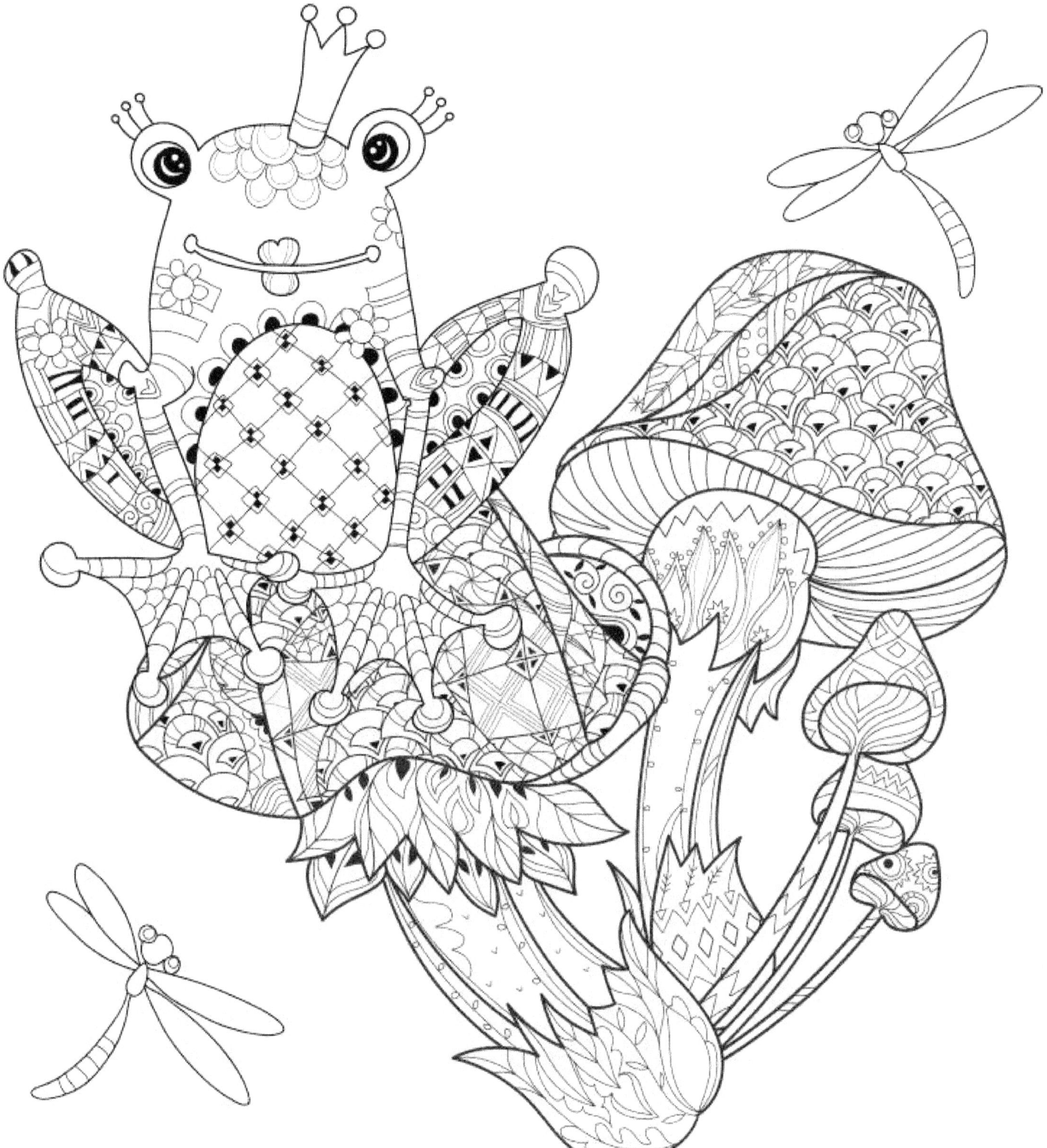

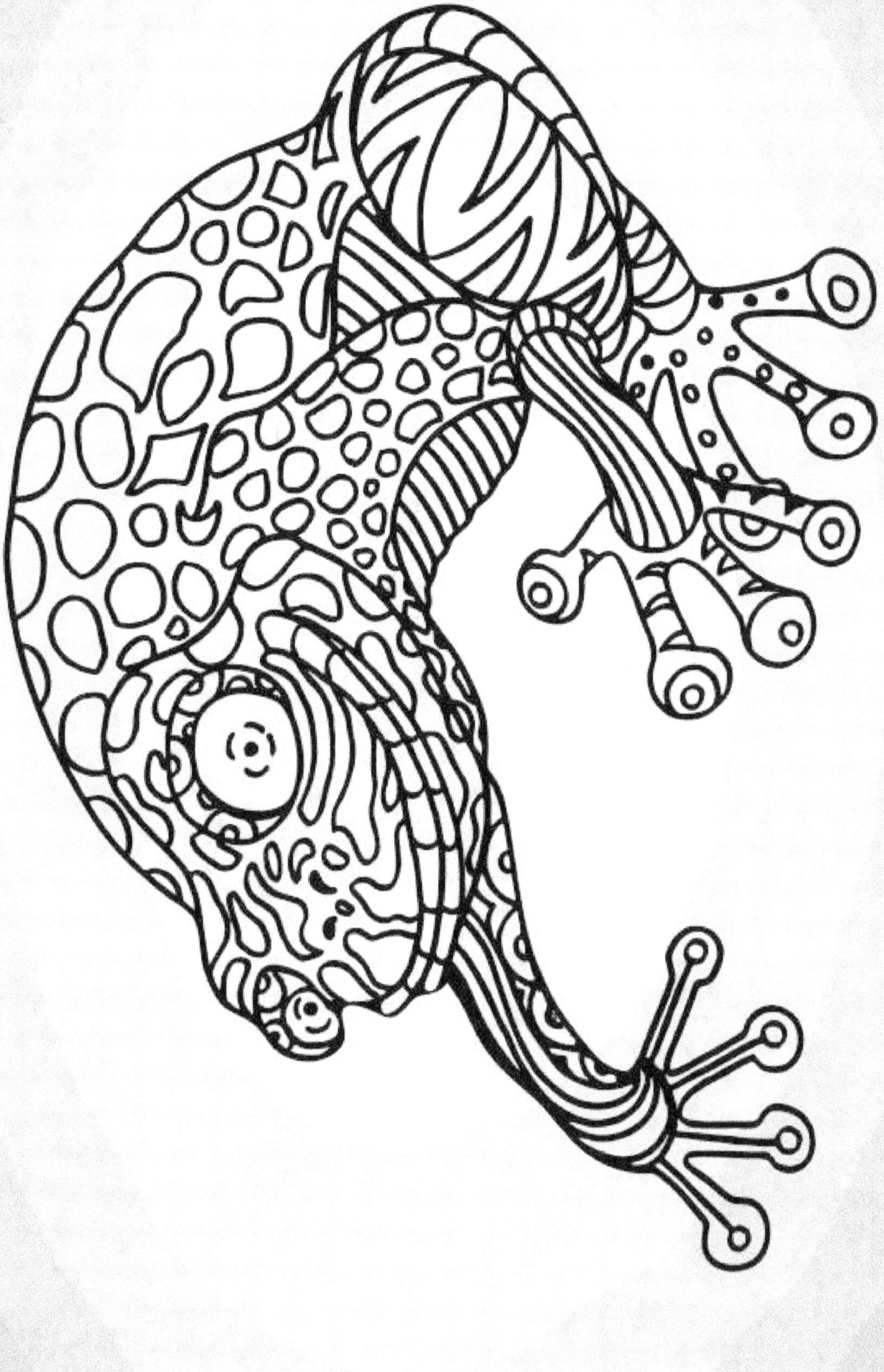

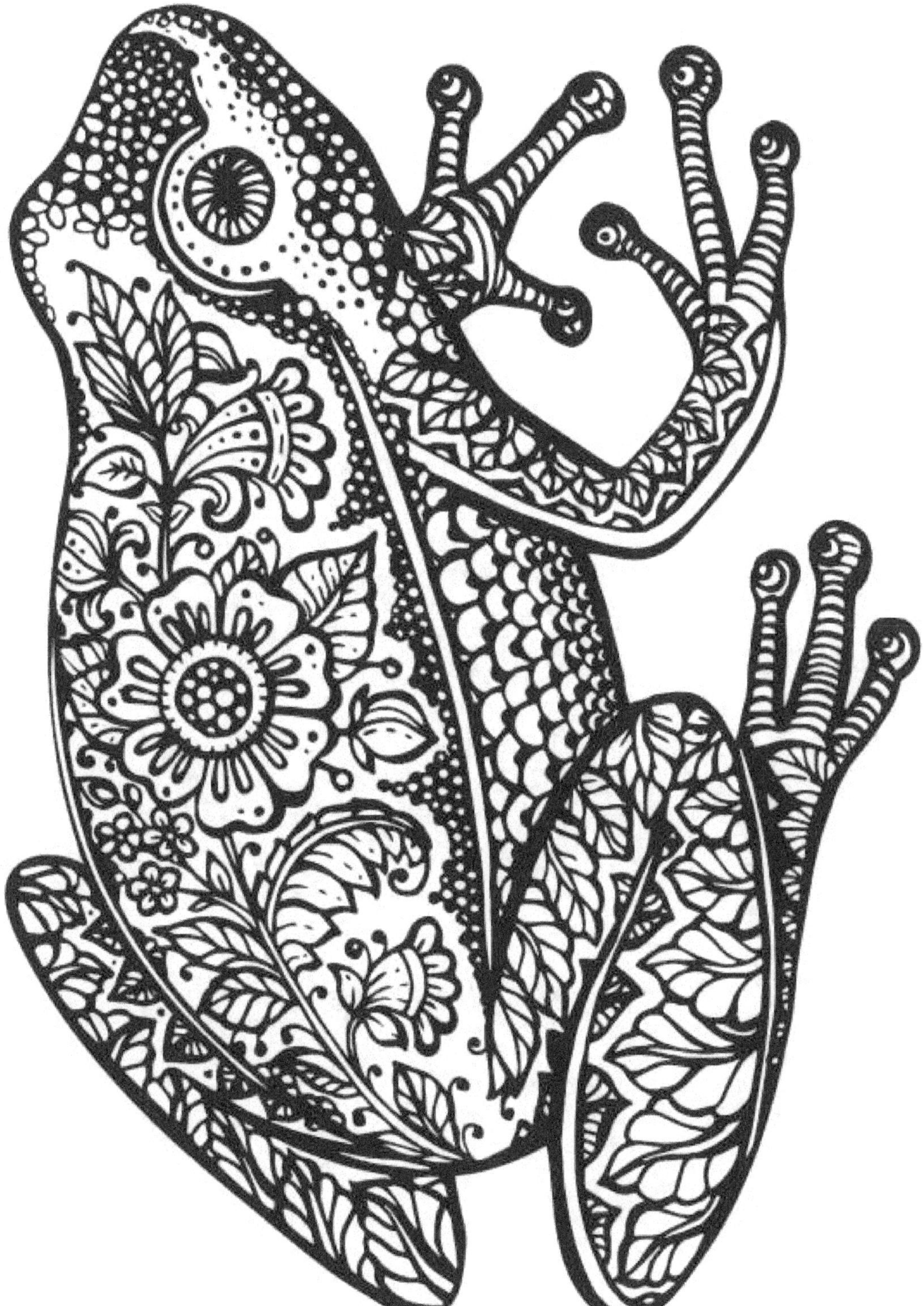

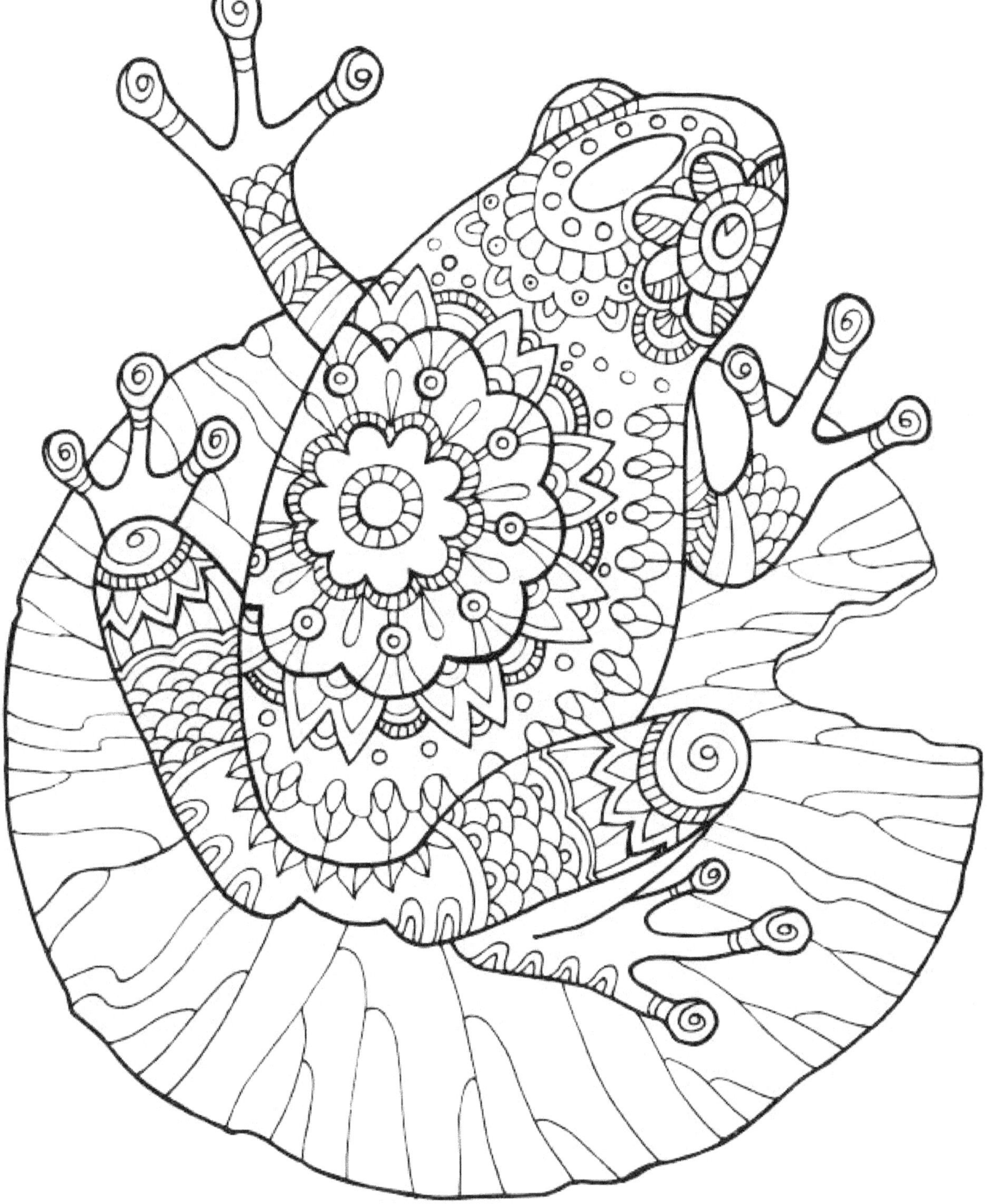

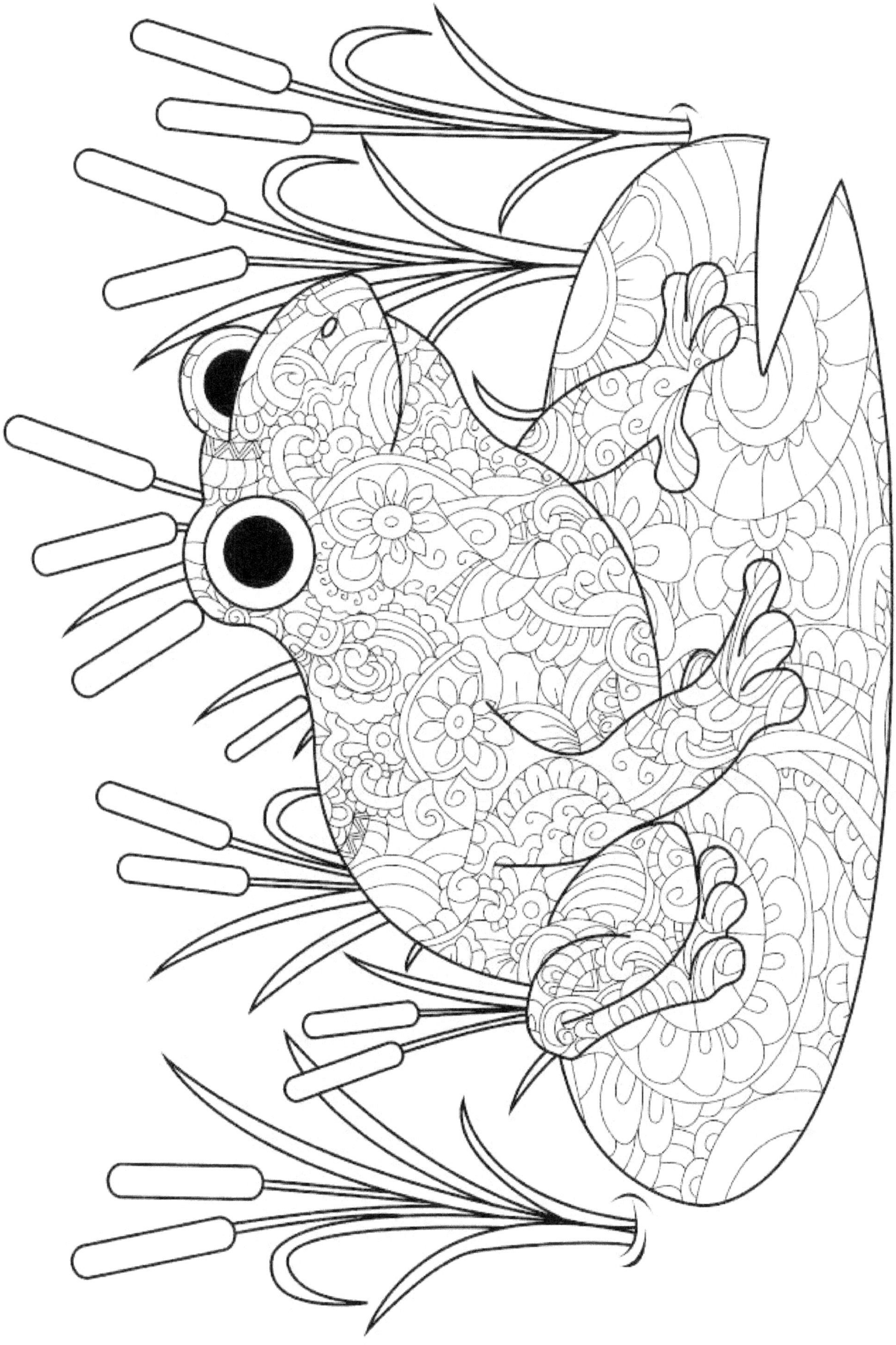

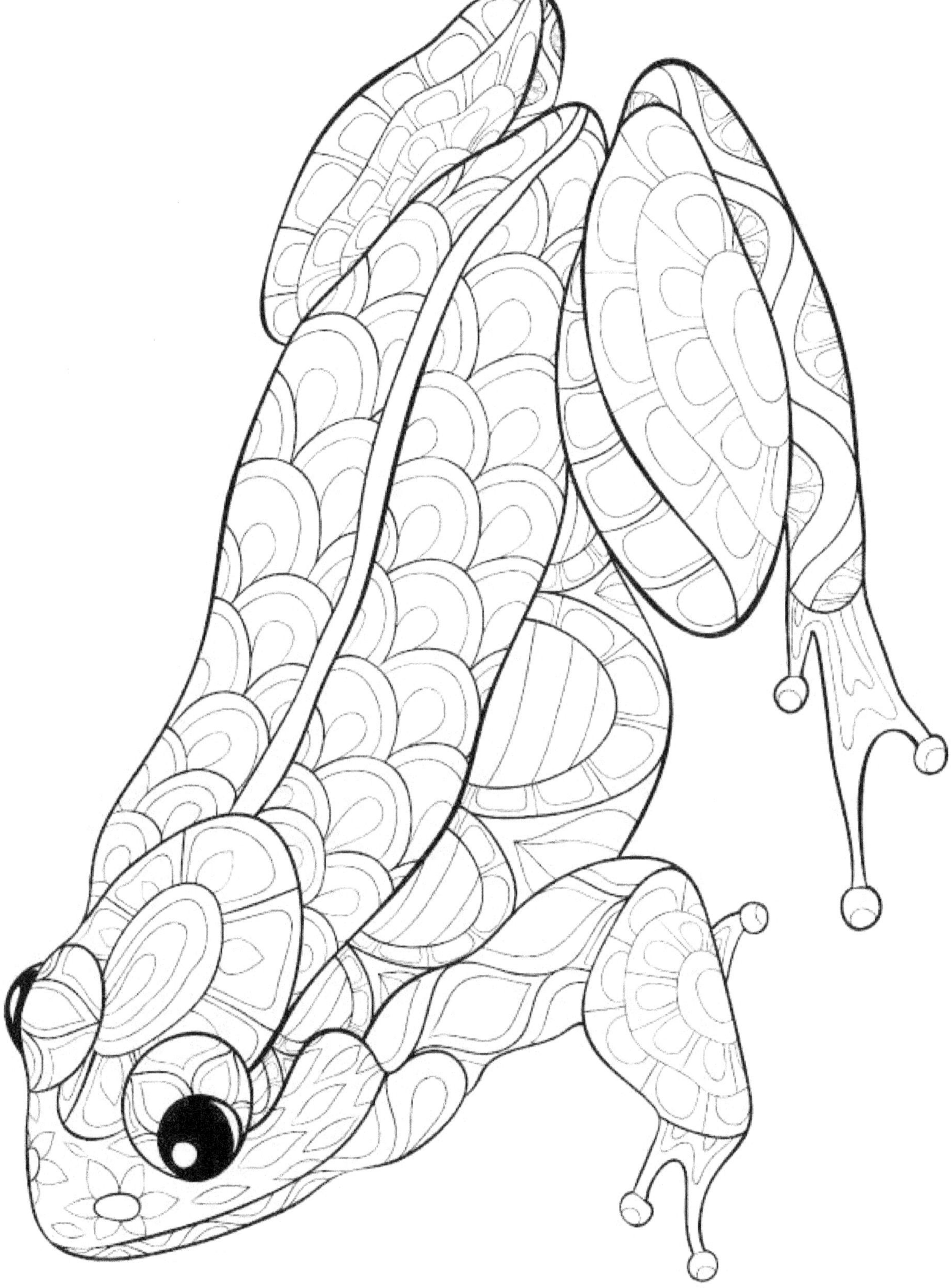

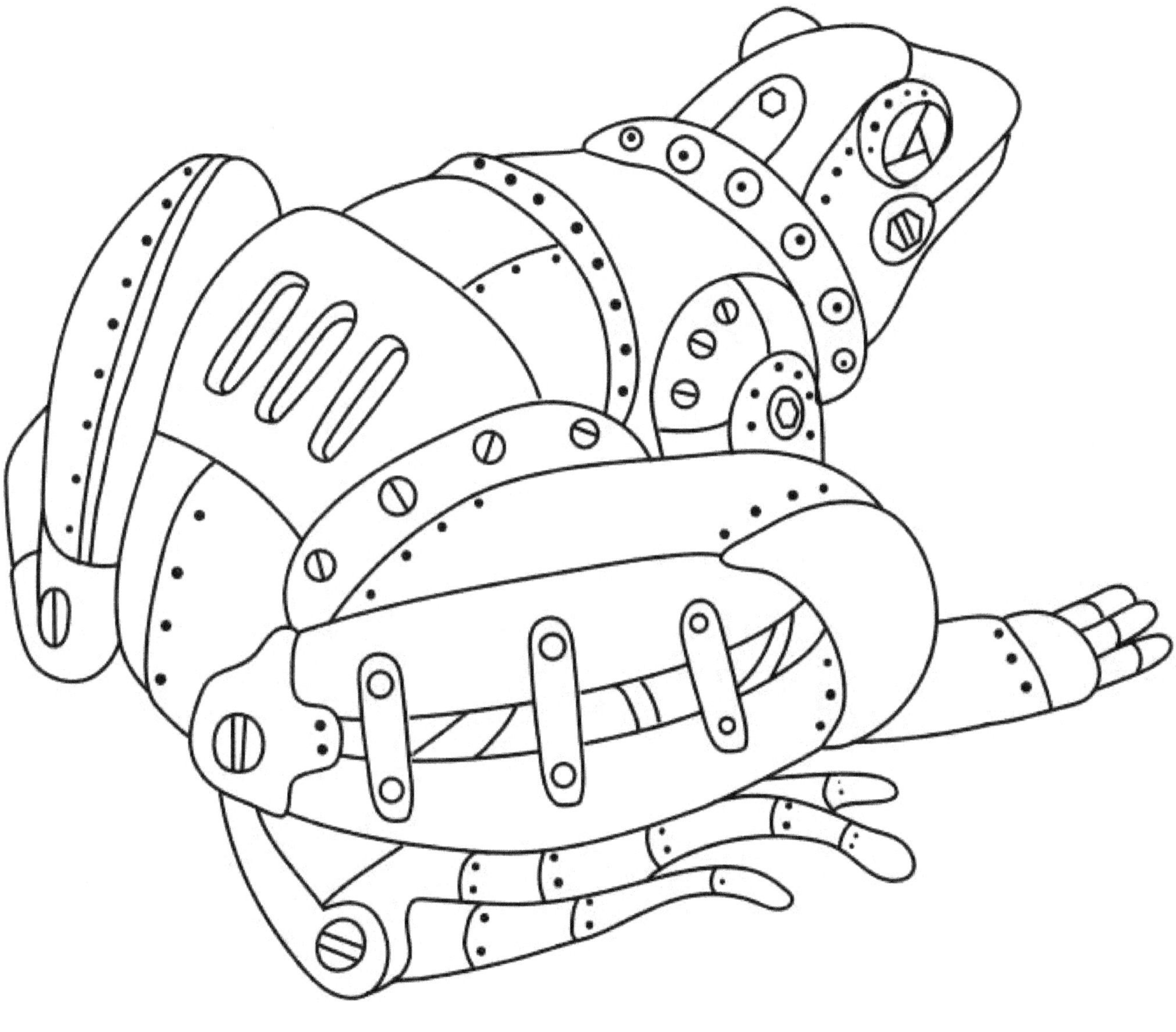

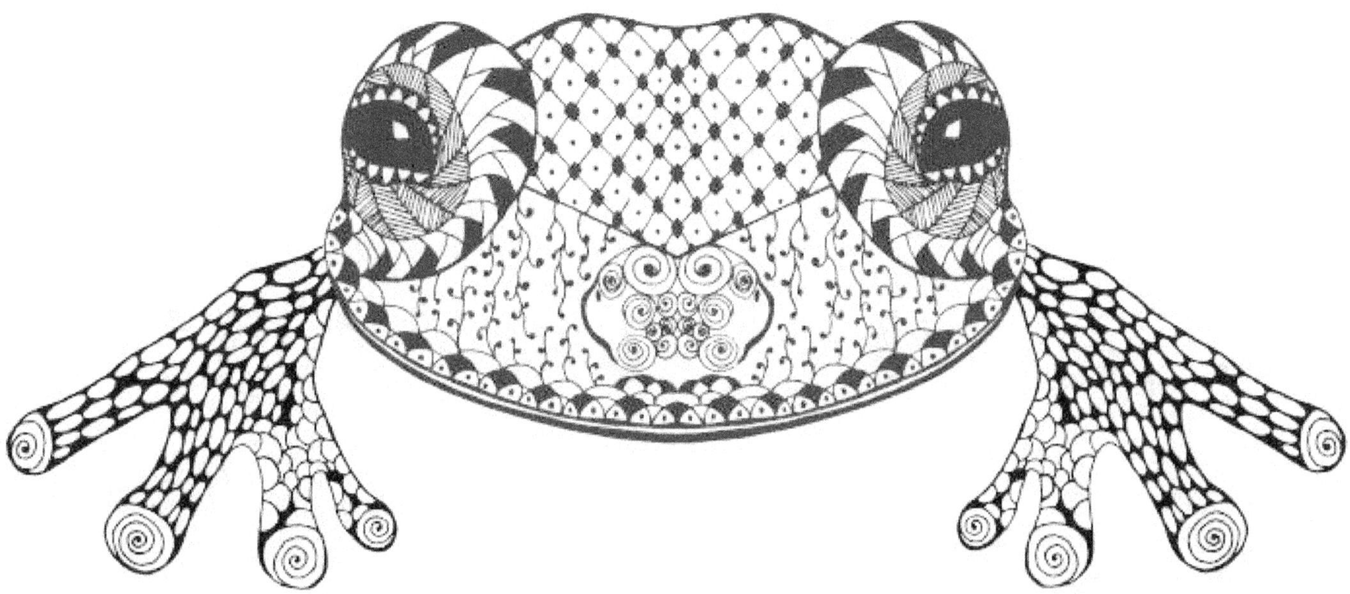

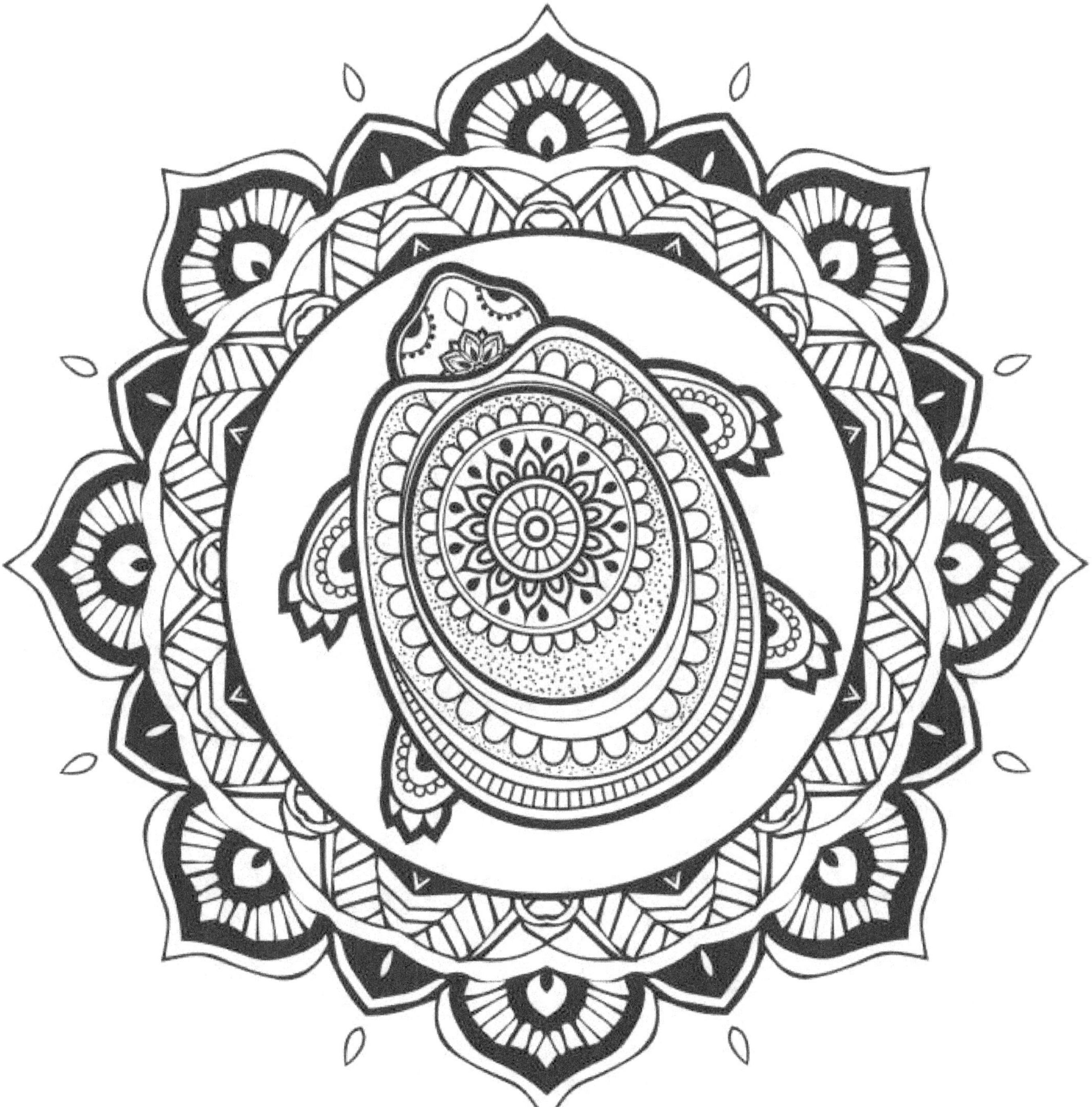

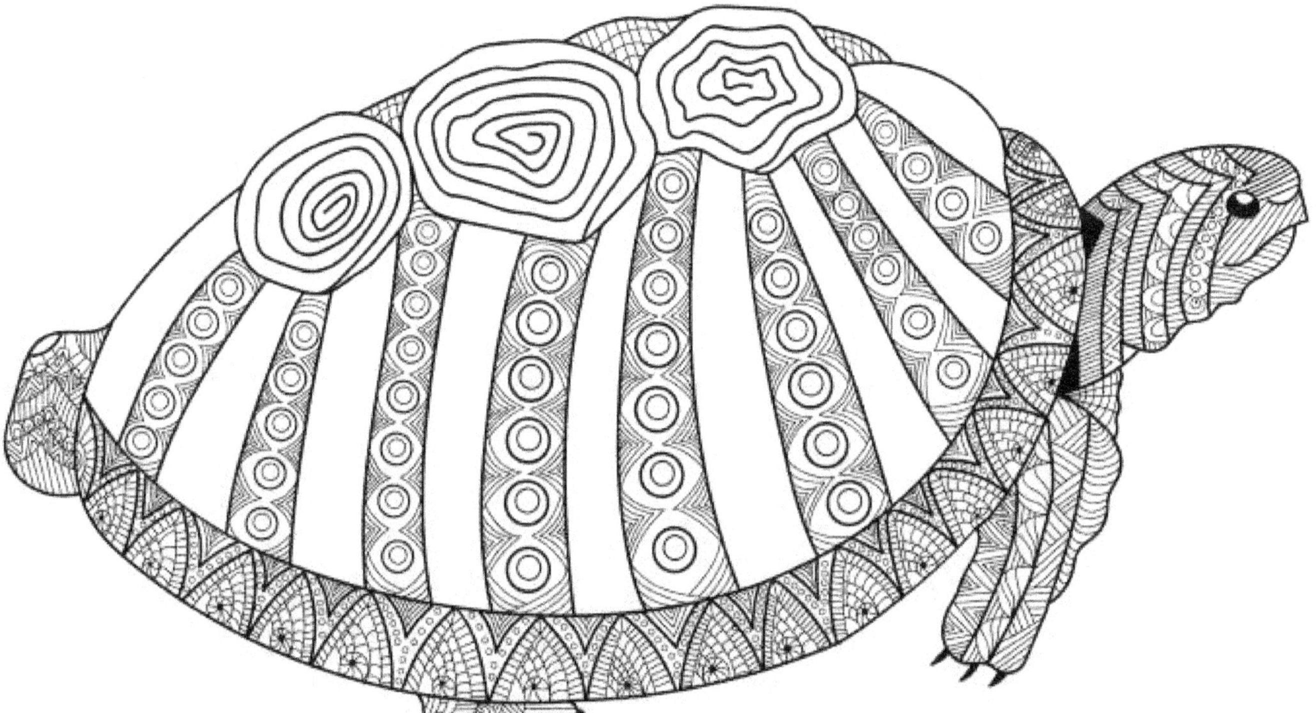

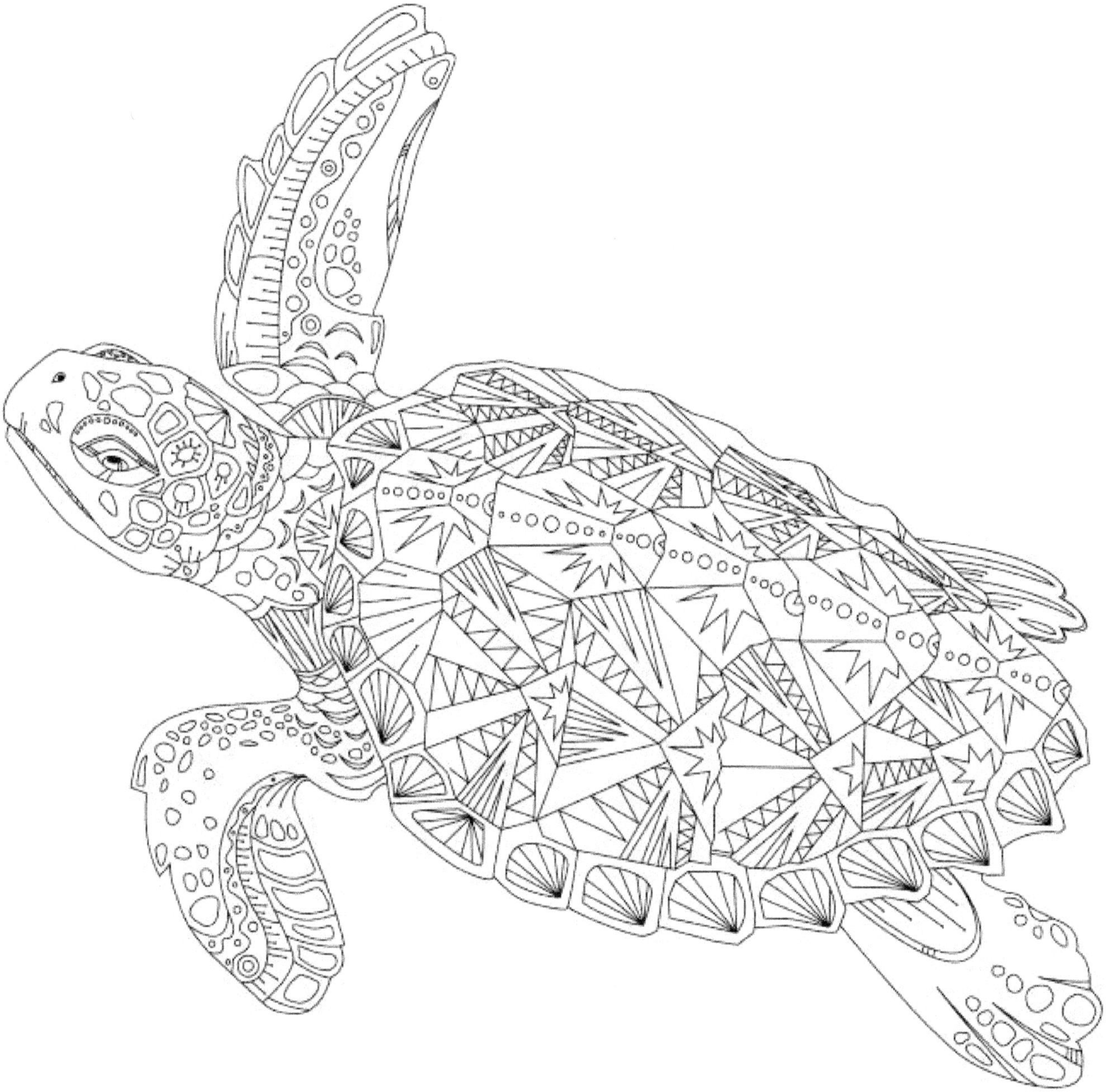

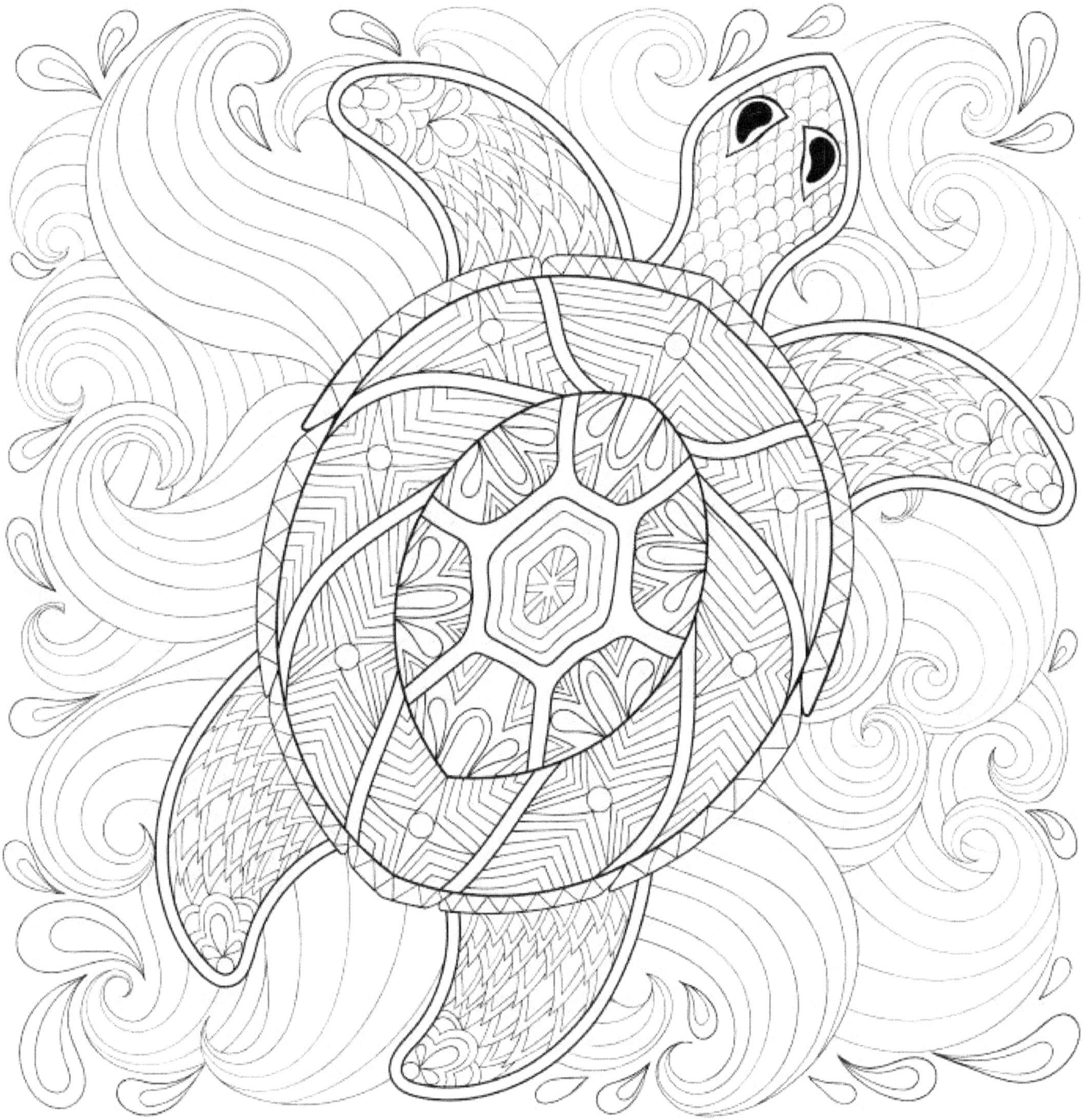

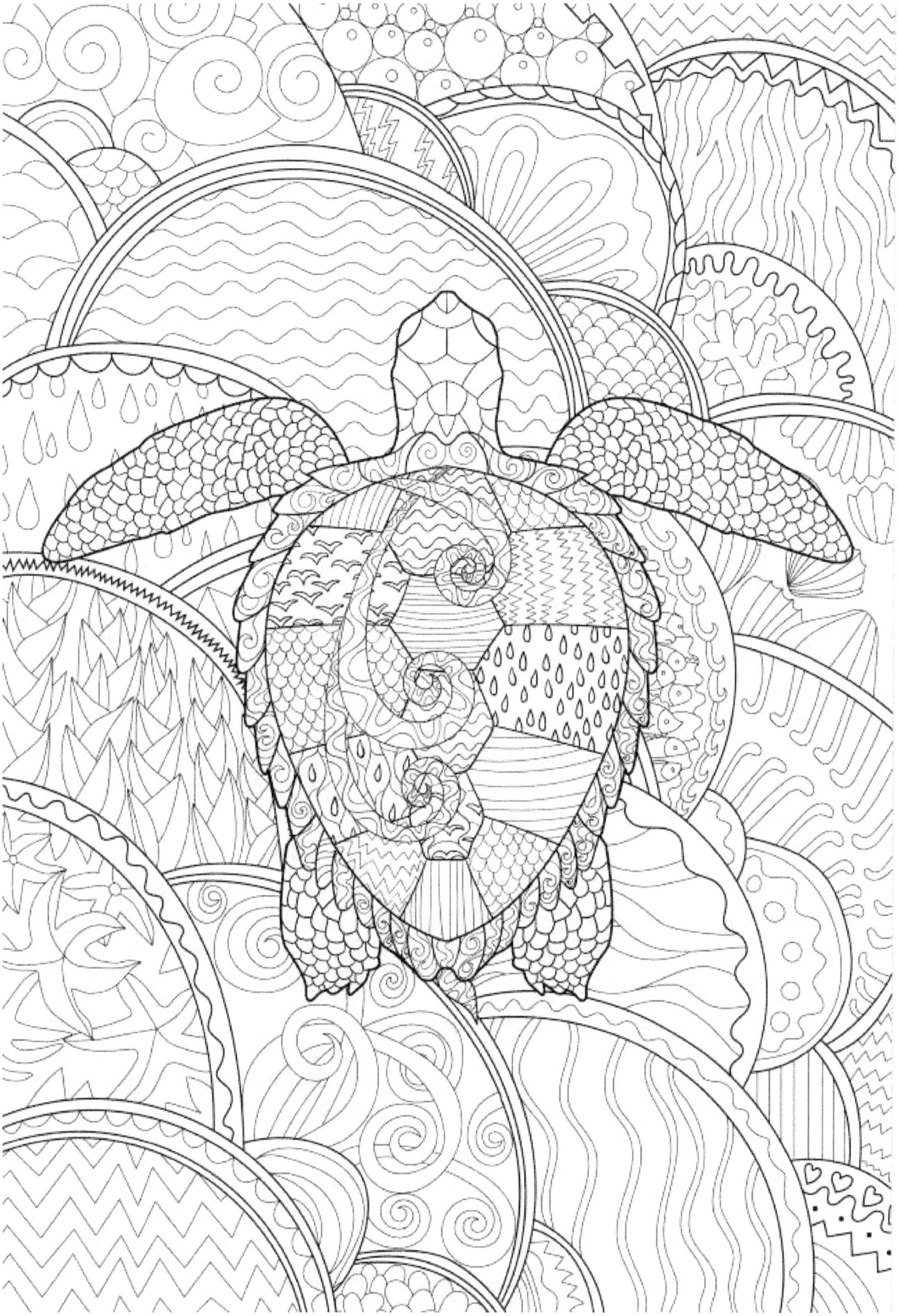

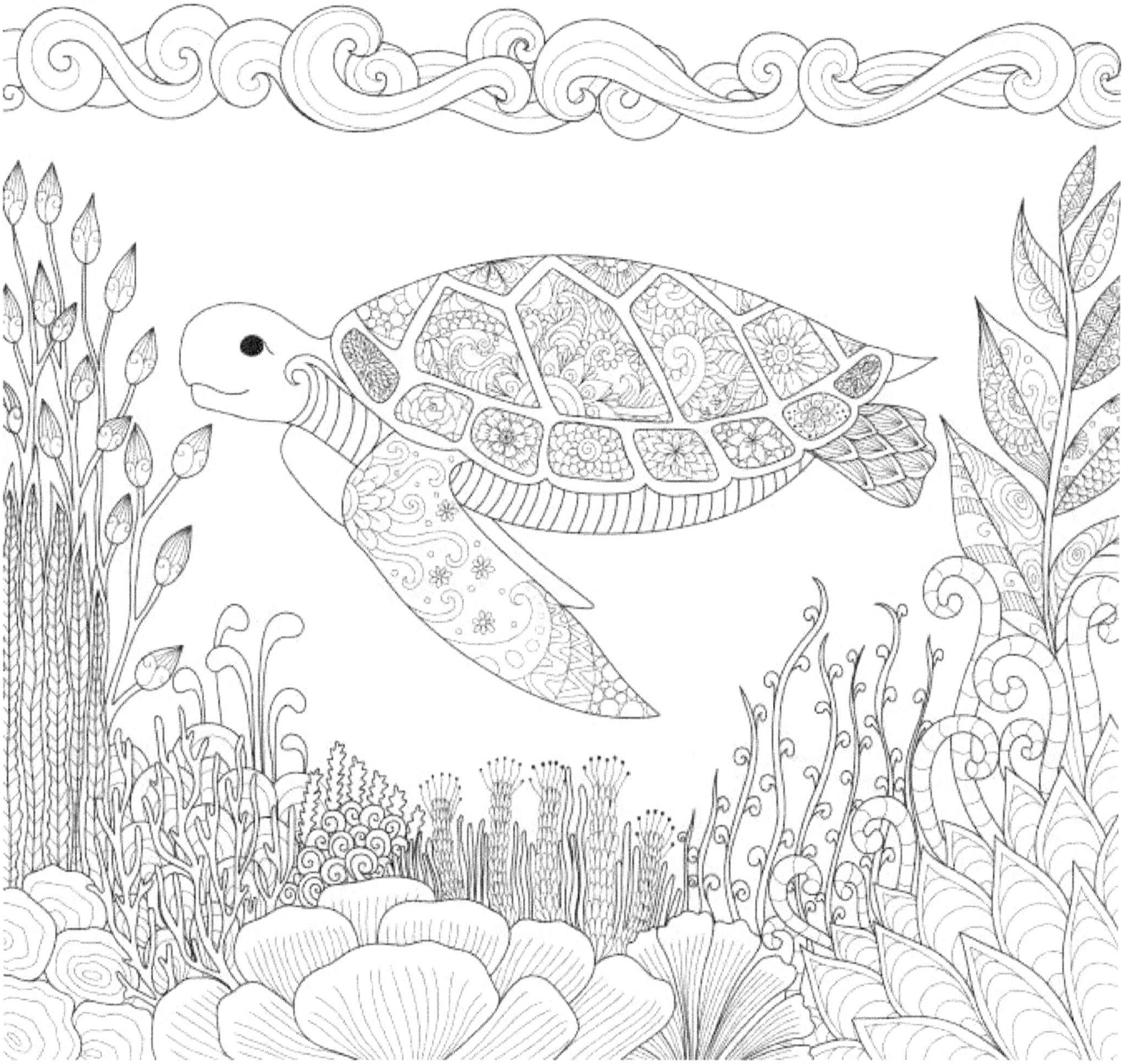

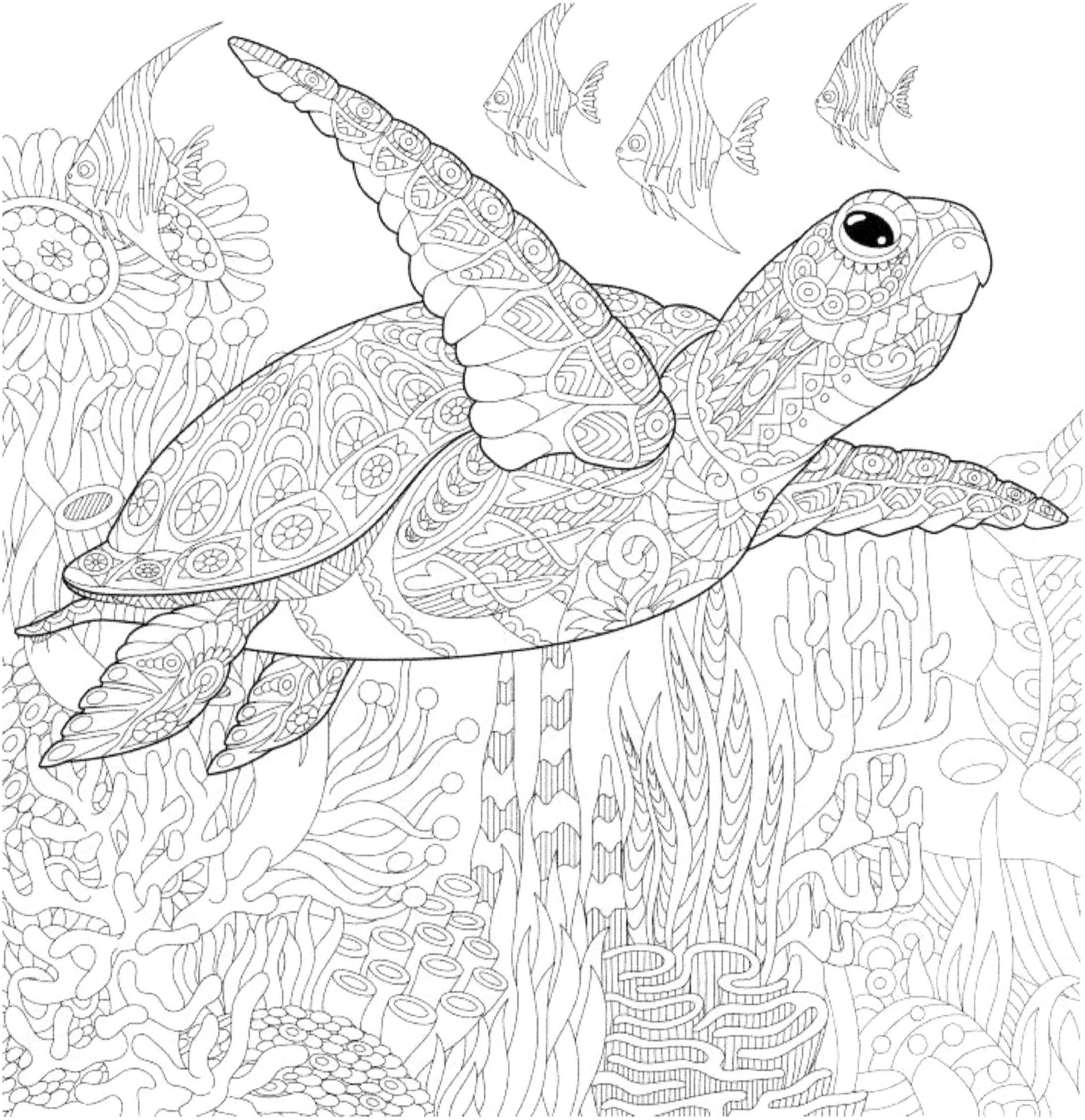

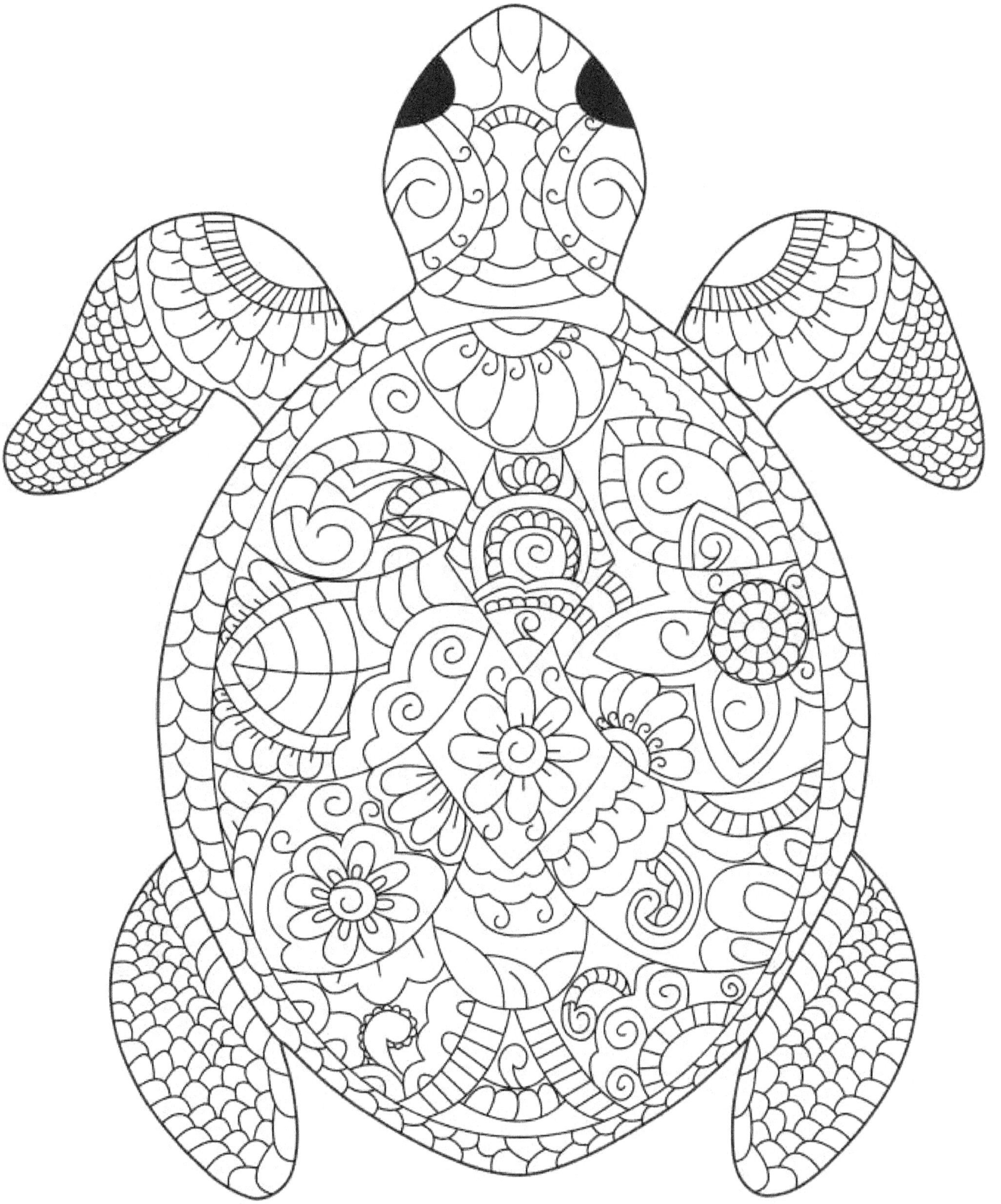

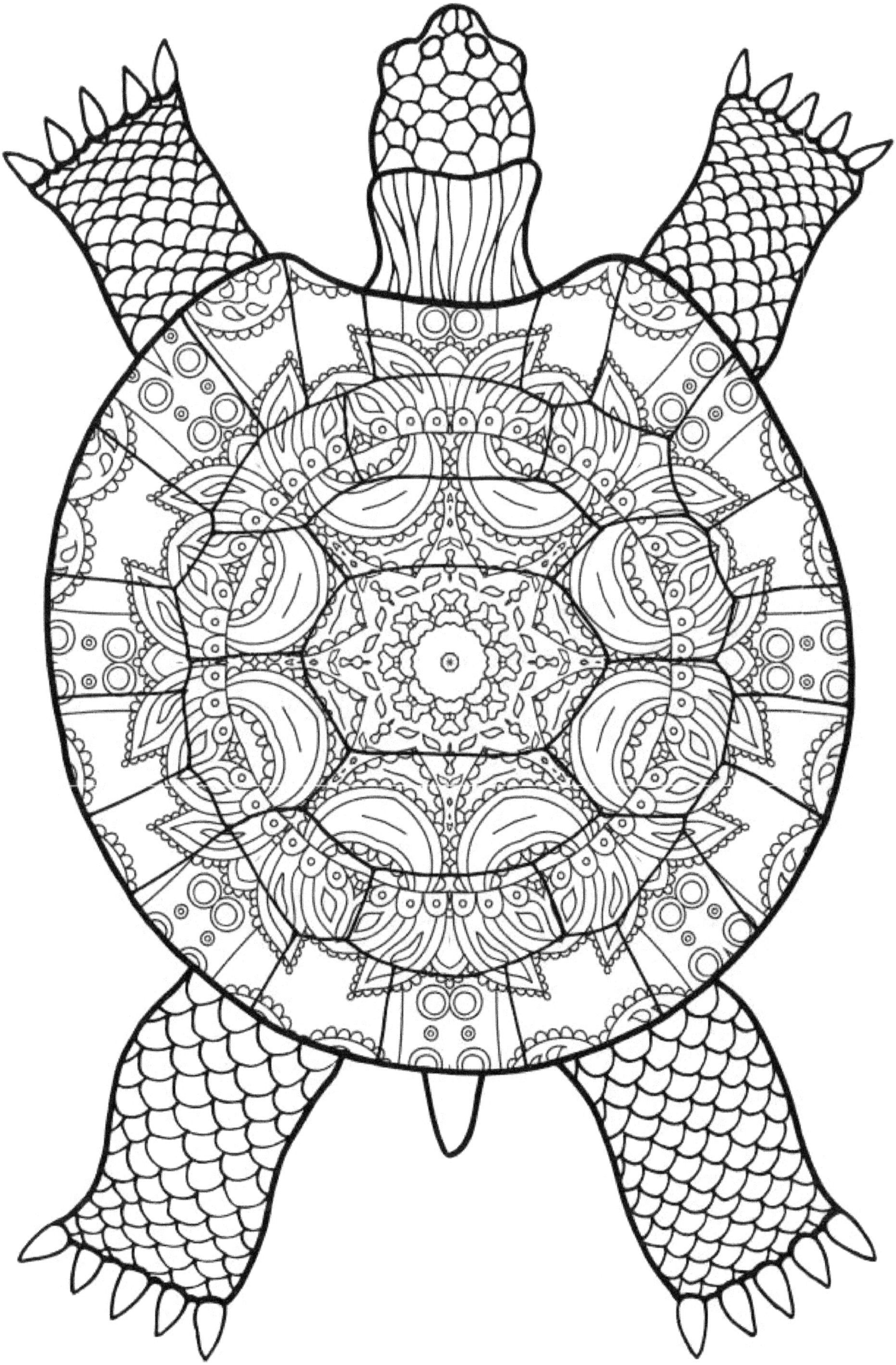

www.ingramcontent.com/pod-product-compliance
Lightning Source LLC
Chambersburg PA
CBHW081216170526
45165CB00009B/2837
* 9 7 8 1 5 4 8 9 5 4 4 5 1 *